The Longest War:
America's Forty Year War on Drugs

BY

CHARLES R. MILLER

2013

INTRODUCTION

In the longest running war in American history, the tables have been turned. After forty years, not only have we been unable to win the War on Drugs, drugs have declared war on us. And they are winning.

"Illegal drugs continue to be harvested no matter how many fields we destroy. New drug cartels are formed as fast as we dismantle them, corruption undermines our police forces as inexorably as moisture destroys walls". [1]

Isabell Patterson, novelist and literary critic once wrote:

"Most of the harm in the world is done by good people, motivated by high ideals towards what they hold to be virtuous ends".

In our Puritan resolve to be tough on crime, we have managed to transform a relatively harmless indulgence from a cottage industry into a global juggernaut controlled by the most brutal and ruthless criminal force in history that every nation on earth, including the United States, has been powerless to stop and will likely never be able to stop. As a noted sociologist said in a study of conflict:

"The dominion of an organized minority, obeying a single impulse, over the unorganized majority is inevitable. A hundred men acting in concert with a common understanding will triumph over one thousand

---

[1] Gustavo Gonazalez-Baez, "Mexico Is Committed to Cooperation with U. S. Drug Prohibition Efforts".
  Drug Legalization, ed. Scott Barbour, (San Diego:Greenhaven Press, 2000) , <http://socialissues.
  wiseto.com/Articles/FO3020630289/> 25 April 2010

i

men who are not in accord and can therefore only be
dealt with one by one".

Over four decades, the sole achievement of the War on
Drugs has been to motivate and empower drug cartels to
vanquish any and all opposition, including the United States.
Nothing we have done has put a dent in the drug trade. Despite
more than 40 million arrests, seven million drug felony
convictions,[2] $2.5 trillion in spending[3] and 1,000 new prisons,[4]
drug trafficking has gone global and is stronger than ever.

We have applied nothing we have learned from fighting
this war. We have ignored all new studies and research and
disregarded practical lessons gleaned from combating drug
trafficking in favor of pursuing policies that do not work and
have not worked in forty years.

We continue treating marijuana as a public health menace
and a "gateway" to harder drug use even though we now know
that marijuana is a relatively harmless substance that is safer than
alcohol and cigarettes. We continue imprisoning record numbers
of generation after generation of our young people, and
destroying countless millions of lives in the process, even though
we know that incarceration does not deter drug use. We continue
spending billions to "fight" drug production and trafficking in
foreign countries and to keep drugs from crossing our borders
even though we know that neither approach is effective and has
only exacerbated drug violence.

Study after study has come to the same conclusion:
military initiatives, interdiction and imprisoning drug users is not

---

[2] Eric E. Sterling, Criminal Justice Policy Foundation, "Opinion: We aren't winning 40 year war on
    Drugs".<http://www.ksl.comid=24545658&nid=757 > 7 May 2013
[3] David W. Fleming and James P. Gray,"This is the U. S. on Drugs", *L. A.
    Times,* July 5, 2008 <http://articles.latimes.com/2008/jul05/
    opinion/oe-fleming5> 7 April 2010
[4] Eric Schlosser, *The Atlantic Magazine",* December, 1998,
<http://www.theatlantic.com/magazine/print/
    1998/12/the-prison-industrial-complex/4669/> 3 May, 2010

only prohibitively expensive, they have no effect on reducing availability, use or demand for drugs. Short of legalizing or decriminalizing drugs, the only proven way to make inroads in decreasing drug use is treatment. According to the RAND Corporation, treatment is 23 times more effective in reducing drug use than interdiction or incarceration and every dollar spent on treatment reduces the costs of crime by more than seven dollars. [5]

Interdiction has had zero effect in keeping illicit drugs from entering our borders. Although the DEA usually estimates a 10% success rate, the truth is we will never have sufficient resources to search, monitor or patrol even 1% of all the possible avenues of drug smuggling. The coastline of British Columbia alone stretches almost 17,000 miles and is virtually uncontrollable. Our border with Mexico stretches almost 2,000 miles and including Alaska, our border with Canada is just over 7,000 contiguous miles. Immigration and customs officials have been overwhelmed by the sheer number of tractor-trailers pouring across the Mexican border as the consequence of NAFTA, many carrying drugs. Upwards of a thousand trucks cross the border in a four hour period. Said a DEA agent in south Texas, "There's no way we're going to catch everything". [6]

To seal off smuggling routes at our Southwestern borders, we put more boots on the ground, increased patrols, used checkpoints, sniffer dogs, cameras, motion detectors, heat sensors, drone aircraft and put up more than 1,000 miles of steel beam, concrete walls and heavy mesh stretching from California to Texas. According to the Office of National Drug Control

---

[5] "Economics", Get the Facts.DrugWarFacts.org, <http://drugwarfacts.org/cms/?q=node/38> 9 April, 2010
[6] Ben Wallace-Wells, "How America Lost the Drug War", *Rolling Stone Magazine,* <http://www.rolling-
Stone.com/politics/news/how-america-lost-the-war-on-drugs-20110324?print+true> 28 April, 2013

Policy, none of that had any effect on stemming the tide of drugs into the U. S.[7]

The United States has 90,000 miles of coast line and 300 ports of entry. Just one busy port receives 100,000 containers a week.[8] Over two million tons of cargo will be handled in major ports across the U. S. on almost a daily basis. Los Angeles will handle over 130,000 containers in a given month. Customs will examine about 440. The other 129,560 will pass through with no inspection whatsoever. The entire yearly shipments of cocaine into the United States would fit into just thirteen of those containers. A single container could hold a years' supply of heroin.[9]

Cracking down on major drug production areas like Colombia, Afghanistan and Mexico has done nothing to stop the availability of drugs. The production simply shifts elsewhere. Afghanistan produces at least 70% of the world's heroin supply. Yet, heroin can also be produced in Asia, the Middle East, Central Asia, China and throughout South America. India is able to produce heroin legally as can Australia. Colombia is the world's major producer of cocaine. Yet, coca plants can also be grown in Peru, Bolivia and Venezuela.

Neither have we been able to shut off trafficking zones and routes. Syria has been involved in drug trafficking for decades. Iran, Pakistan, Indonesia, Somalia, Algeria and Chechnya are involved in drug trafficking as is Cuba, Ecuador, Paraguay, Argentina, Brazil, Venezuela and all throughout Central America.[10] To think we can police every square mile of

---

[7] Fox News, <http://www.foxnews.com/world/2010/05/13/ap-impact-of-years-trillion-war-drugs-failed-
  to-meet-goals/> 23 April, 2013
[8] "Drug War: Covert Money, Power & Policy: Interdiction", Drugwar.com. <http://www.drugwar.com/
  interdiction.shtm> 27 April, 2013
[9] Mike Gray, "Drug Crazy", p. 5151-152
[10] Rachael Ehrenfeld, Director – American Center for Democracy & the New York City Center for the

the globe to interdict drug trafficking is naïve at best and arrogant at worst. The Hullaga Valley of Colombia alone covers an area three times the size of Massachusetts.[11] Yet we continue spending billions of dollars of tax payer money on interdiction every year and have been doing so for four decades.

Our war on drugs has produced two disastrous consequences that are far worse than college kids smoking pot. The first has been to transform the United States from the moral leader in the human rights movement, to the world leader among all nations in the absolute number of its citizens serving time behind bars and the per capita rate at which it imprisons its citizens. The greatest democracy in the history of mankind imprisons more people and at a higher rate than the worst dictatorships and despotic governments, including Russia and China.[12]

The second consequence has been to fuel a flickering flame of drug trafficking into a raging inferno. What was once a regionally based system of mom and pop drug dealers and distributors has been corporatized on a global scale by drug cartels in strategic response to the escalation of interdiction efforts imposed by the War on Drugs. It was a natural evolution, the Darwinian theory of "survival of the fittest". To survive, the drug trade had to find a way to counter intensified interdiction. As a result, drug trafficking has exploded into a $400 billion enterprise that has penetrated every corner of the globe and infiltrated all major cities around the world, including the United States.[13] Drug profits are nourishing terrorist groups who,

Study of Corruption and the rule of the Law (CSC)., New York, USA., Workshop held at Los Alamos

National Laboratory March 25-29, "Funding Terrorism: Sources and Methods.

[11] Mike Gray, "Drug Crazy", (Random House New York), 1998, p. 114

[12] "Drug War Prisoner Count Over Half a Million", Stop The Drug War, <http://stopthedrugwar.org/
chronicle-old/409/toohigh.shtml> 22 April 2010

[13] Associated Press, "U. N. Estimates Drug Business Equal to 8 Percent of World Trade" (June 26, 1997),

because of their insatiable need for funds, are now in league with drug syndicates. Trumping that threat, organized crime, i.e., the Mafia and other international crime organizations, are seeking their slice of the money pie, and have formed mutually beneficial alliances with drug dealers and terrorists.

Drug cartels have defied every attempt to put them out of business. They possess modern technology and military grade weaponry that often exceeds that of local law enforcement and has made the cartels stronger and more formidable than ever.[14] Mexican drug cartels have recruited paramilitary forces that are better trained, better equipped and more loyal than the Mexican Army. [15] Drug trafficking organizations have been successful in intimidating or corrupting any opposition through threats, assassinations and bribes. They have been successful in destabilizing national economies and disrupting orderly processes of sovereign governments. This is the legacy of our War on Drugs.

< http://ww w.drugpolicy.org/library/factsheets/economiccons/fact_economic.cfm> 9 April, 2010

[14] "Drug Trafficking Overview", Wise to Social Issues, <http://socialissues.wiseto.com/Articles/ FO3020640073> 25 April 2010

[15] Patrick Cooley, "The Mexican Drug War and How it Affects the United States", April 13, 2009, <http:internationalaffairs.suite101.com/article.cfm/the_mexican_drug_war> 7 April, 2010

CHAPTER ONE

Futility of the Drug War

The Drug War has failed, and will continue to fail, for one simple reason. It ignores the basic principles of elementary economics: the law of supply and demand. We are attacking the wrong end of the equation. Prohibition and interdiction attempt to curtail the supply side. All that does is limit supply in the face of continued demand which only increases profits for drug dealers.

Entrepreneurial criminals will navigate around laws and across borders to meet the demand for illegal goods and services whether it be for drugs, human kidneys, human beings, weapons or rhinoceros horns. As long as someone is willing to buy it, someone will be willing to sell it.[16]

This is why no matter how much we spend on interdiction, as long as the demand for drugs continues, there will always be those willing to satisfy that demand, no matter the risk. First of all, the profits are simply too huge. It costs about $4,000 to $5,000 to produce a kilo of heroin. That kilo will sell for $250,000 to $300,000 *wholesale,* or 50 times the production cost. The U. S. State Department estimates that over 500 metric tons of heroin were sold in 2001 at a street value of at least $30 billion.[17] That's just one drug.

---

[16] Jeremy Hanken, "Transnational Crime in the Developing World", Global Financial Integrity, Washington, D. C. Center for International Policy, February, 2011, no. 268, p. 6.

[17] "Funding Terrorism: Sources and Methods", Rachael Ehrenfeld, Director, American Center for

   Democracy & the New York City Center for the Study of Corruption and the rule of Law (CSC),

   New York, USA, Workshop held at Los Alamos National Laboratory March 25-29, 2002

   <http://artcles.latimes.com/2011/jul/10/world/la-fg-mexico-violence-20110110> 4 May 2013

Second of all, losing drugs in shipment does not affect drug dealers because most drugs are not shipped until they have been paid. According to a former DEA agent, the drug trade is so lucrative and obscenely profitable, even if interdiction resulted in intercepting and seizing 90% of drug shipments, a cartel would still make a killing on the 10% that got through.[18]

Last and most important, the illicit drug trade is THE most reliable source of income in the world with a demand that continues to grow.[19] No other commodity, legal or illegal, that exists today can match the profits and returns of illegal drugs.[20] And it's all tax free. After forty years of failure, one would think we would have figured out by now that the economics of the illegal drug trade are simply too compelling to be overcome by conventional means.

To better illustrate the huge amounts of dollars that are at stake, the world market for drugs is estimated to be a $400 billion a year international industry, or 8% of total world trade. Americans spend about $60 billion yearly on drugs.[21] Imagine if you were a drug dealer and your organization only got one tenth of 1% of those expenditures. You would *only* have made $60 million for your troubles. And the U. S. represents only about 15% of the total world market for illegal narcotics.[22]

This is why drug traffickers will spare no dime and assume even more risk to continue moving their merchandise no matter how stringent interdiction becomes. They can simply pass their incremental distribution costs, i.e., the added expense of circumventing increasingly sophisticated interdiction measures, on to the ultimate consumer. Buyers will gladly pay the higher

---

[18] "Do the Math", PBS,
<http://www.pbs.org/wgbh/pages/frontline/shows/drugs/special/math.htnl>
   30 April 2013
[19] Ibid
[20] Ibid
[21] "Drug Trafficking Overview"
[22] International Drug Control Cooperation,
<https://www.ncjrs.gov/ondcppubs/publications/policy/
   99ndcs/iv-h..html> 10 May 2013

price because the marginal cost to them is negligible. The foregoing reasons are why efforts to stop the flow of illegal drugs into the United States are doomed never to work. The proof is the failed forty year history of the War on Drugs.

An honest assessment of the drug war paints a bleak picture of its inability to reduce the flow of illegal drugs. Demand is simply too strong and profits too lucrative to pass up. But that isn't the total picture of what's wrong with the drug war. The real picture is much worse. In fact, the *use* of illicit drugs isn't even the problem. The problem is making use of drugs illegal. That gives rise to a Black Market, which in turn, attracts criminal elements to fill the void.

We've been misled about the so-called dangers of drugs thanks to years of exaggerated propaganda, unfounded prejudices, misconceptions and dissembling on the part of elected officials anxious to appear tough on crime. None of this has helped educate and enlighten the American public as to the problems created by drug prohibition and how it can be solved.

Failed political leadership is the number one cause of the global trafficking scourge. With each misstep in its War on Drugs, the government's response has been like that of the man who tried to dig himself out of a hole. All he accomplished was to dig even deeper the hole he was in. For example, in 1980 – nine years after President Nixon declared war on drugs - the nation spent about one billion dollars on drug control. In 2013, that amount is conservatively estimated at between $50 to $70 billion from state and federal sources combined. [23] So the hole gets deeper and will continue doing so as long as our government keeps pressing a failed strategy and wasting hundreds of billions of our tax dollars in a cause they know is hopelessly lost.

The real tragedy of the drug war is the collateral damage spawned by its wake. Like the shock wave of an atomic blast, the destructive forces unleashed by the War on Drugs have

---

[23] Infelicitious Forty: The Anniversary of the U. S. War on Drugs
<http://www/coha.org/the-
anniversary-of-the-us-war-on-drugs/> 24 April 2013

reverberated across the face of the entire globe. The devastation is incalculable and will continue to increase until political leaders have the courage to attack the problem at its source by removing the profit factor from trafficking. Until that happens, the trafficking juggernaut will not be stopped:

- Just as Prohibition created a Black Market for alcohol that gave birth to organized crime in this country, the Drug War has created drug trafficking and ruthless drug cartels that have defied all measures for eliminating. We finally came to our senses with Prohibition. We haven't with the War on Drugs.

- International drug cartels present the greatest challenge to law enforcement of any other criminal group in history. They are too large, too wealthy, too powerful and too well organized. As soon as one is broken up, another takes its place. Drug trafficking underwrites global terrorism and is the primary source of funds for terrorist groups like Al Qaeda.

- The relentless growth of the drug trafficking industry, and the violence and corruption that inevitably ensues from it, has contributed to destabilizing the economies of countries and disrupting orderly processes of national governments. Colombia, Honduras, El Salvador and Mexico are prime examples.

- Corruption is rampant within law enforcement and justice systems at every level of local, state and national government around the world, including the United States, due to the pervasive influence of drug traffickers and the enormous sums of money at their disposal.

- Alone among Western nations, the United States has elected imprisonment for drug offenses rather than fines and community service as many countries have done. Consequently, prison populations and rates of incarceration are at record levels in the United States because we treat drug use and addiction as crimes rather than relatively harmless indulgences or medical problems.

- Virtual decimation of several generations of young men between the ages of 17 to 30 who can be imprisoned for five or ten years for relatively innocuous, non-violent drug offenses. Because they can be branded as a criminal felon for the rest of their life, finding gainful employment can be almost impossible. Besides needlessly destroying the lives of these young people, we are creating a permanent subculture of people who will always live on the margins of society because they have few alternatives.

- Hundreds of billions of tax dollars have been diverted from education, defense, Social Security, Medicare, infrastructure repairs and paying down a record deficit in order to fund the War on Drugs and its ancillary consequences. In the decade of the 1990s, many states spent more money on prisons than universities. Between 1987 and 2007, inflation adjusted total spending by states on corrections increased by 127% while spending on higher education increased by 21%.[24] Between 1980 and 2000, Texas spent seven dollars on corrections for every dollar spent on higher education.[25]

---

[24] Pew's Center on the State, The Public Safety Performance, p. 15
[25] Texas Tough, Fast Facts <http://texastough.com/resources/facts/> 8 May 2013

- Invasion of the United States by powerful drug cartels who have set up cells in virtually every major city in the nation and in hundreds of smaller communities for the purpose of extending their reach, influence and power on American soil.

CHAPTER TWO

Brief History of Drug Use in America

One must ask exactly how we got ourselves into this mess in the first place. For over two hundred years, despite the open availability of many substances we have now outlawed, the United States somehow grew, prospered, won wars, and managed to become the greatest super power in the history of the world without having to declare a drug menace.

Mood altering drugs have been used by mankind in virtually every civilization since the beginning of recorded history. Yet, nations and geopolitical regions such as Europe, China, Japan, India, the Middle East and Meso-America were able to build advanced civilizations despite unchecked access to mind and mood altering substances.

Opiates have been used recreationally almost since the beginning of recorded history. In 3,400 BC, it was cultivated in Mesopotamia and was referred to as the "joy plant". The art of culling opium from poppy plants was passed from the Sumerians to the Assyrians to the Babylonians to the Egyptians.[26] Around 330 BC, Alexander the Great introduced opium to Persia.[27] In the 8th century A.D., Arab traders brought opium to India and China. From there, it found its way to Europe and Asia Minor.[28] Between 400 – 300 BC, it was widely used by the Arabs, Greeks and Romans. In 1527, one of the fathers of modern medicine, Paracelsus, reintroduced opium to European medical literature as laudanum which was prescribed as a painkiller.[29] In 1680, an English apothecary, Thomas Sydenham, produced Sydenham's

---

[26] "Opiate History" <http://www.opiates.com/opiates/opiate-history.html>
[27] Ibid
[28] Ibid
[29] "A Brief History of Drugs", Lycaeum.org <http://lycaeum.org/-sky/data/drughist.html> 28 April, 2013

Laudanum, a compound of opium, sherry wine and herbs, which quickly became a popular remedy for numerous ailments. [30]

Morphine was the first alkaloid isolated from opium in 1806 by Friedrich Sertuerner of Pladerborn, Germany.[31] Within half a century, dozens more alkaloids were isolated, including atropine, caffeine, cocaine and quinine. The commercial distribution of morphine began in 1827 by E. Merck and Company of Darmstadt, Germany. Morphine was believed to be a non-addictive substitute for alcoholism and widely prescribed for that purpose until the late 1930s.[32]

In 1898, a chemist named Heinrich Dresser with the Bayer Company of Elberfeld, Germany, discovered an extract of morphine that did not have morphine's side effects. Employees who tried the extract said it made them feel "great" or "heroic". The new drug was dubbed Heroin. Three years later Bayer introduced heroin, touting it as a non-addictive substitute for morphine. [33]

Cocaine, as it occurs in the coca plant, has been used for approximately 5,000 years by South American Indians. [34] Spanish conquerors brought the plant back to Europe where it was cultivated by the Catholic Church. The active alkaloid ingredient of the coca plant was first isolated in 1860 by Albert Niemann, a chemist who named the compound Cocaine. [35]Cocaine quickly became popular and was widely used, often mixed with cigarettes and wine. Physicians dispensed it as an antidote to morphine addiction. Cocaine is likely the most profitable of all illicit drugs for drug traffickers. A single gram

---

[30] Ibid

[31] "Opiate History"

[32] Elaine Casey, "History of Drug Use and Drug Users in the United States", Schaffer Library of Drug Policy, <http://www.druglibrary.org/schaffer/history/casey1.htm > 22 April, 2010

[33] "A Brief History of Drugs"

[34] "The History of Cocaine" <http://www.a1b2c3.com/drugs/coc01.htm> 3 May, 2013

[35] Ibid

costs less than one dollar to produce in Colombia but sells for $80 in the United States.

Prior to the 1880s, there were no drug laws in the United States and laws subsequently passed were not seriously enforced until the 1920s. In the 1880s, patent medicines and opium preparations such as Dover's Powder were extremely popular. Laudanum (opium mixed with alcohol) was cheaper than beer or wine and quickly became a favorite of lower paid workers. While there was abuse and addictions, there is no evidence that abuse was so excessive as to be a national medical or social concern.

In the late 19th and early 20th century, a vast array of over-the-counter patent medicines were laced with everything from morphine to opium to cocaine. A popular cough syrup spiked with heroin was available by mail-order.[36] A century ago, opium was widely used in the American west. In the latter part of the 19th century, opiate consumption (morphine and heroin) was commonplace due to the prescribing and dispensing of legal opiates by physicians to women with "female problems" (typically menstrual cramping) and the popularity of patent medicines such as Laudenum that was flavored with opiates. It is estimated that during that era the number of opiate addicts was approximately 150,000 to 250,000, with between two-thirds and three-quarters being women.[37] On a per capita basis, this is twice as high as the number of opiate addicts today.[38] Amphetamines were first synthesized in 1887 by the drug company Smith, Kline and French but not marketed until 1932. Because of its "stimulant" qualities, it was widely dispensed by the military on both sides to keep soldiers alert. [39] Doctors across the country

---

[36] Mike Gray, "Drug Crazy", (Random House, New York, 1998) , p. 43
[37] "Prohibition (Drugs)", <http://en.wikipedia.org/wiki/Prohibition_(drugs)> 18 April, 2013
[38] Ibid
[39] "Amphetamines – History"
<http://science.jrank.org/pages/302/Amphetamines-History.html,>
    28 April, 2013

prescribed such medications to individuals with addiction problems freely and without reproach. Some of the more popular sellers were substances now outlawed: [40]

1. Opium – Sold in the 19th century as Laudanum, a tincture of alcohol mixed with opium.
2. Cannabis – Grown freely until the early 20th century. First laws passed in 1906 but no sentences handed out until 1940s.
3. Amphetamines – Benzendrine (or "bennies") used in inhalers and tablets and available over the counter until the 1950s.
4. Methamphetamines – Street name crystal meth, ice or glass. Used as an active ingredient in Sudafed.
5. Amyl Nitrates – Know as "poppers". Until 1960 could be obtained without a prescription.
6. Codeine – Opium derivative extracted from morphine, isolated in 1832 by a French chemist named Pierre Robiquet. Active ingredient in cough syrups until relatively recently.
7. Cocaine –Could be easily obtained at any pharmacy. Used as active ingredient in toothache powders. Used in initial manufacture of Coca-Cola. Sold by pharmacies as ingredient in cigarettes. Not outlawed until 1914.
8. Quaaludes – Synthesized in India in 1951 as a safe alternative to barbiturates. Appeared in U. S. as a sedative in 1965 until prohibited in 1973.
9. Heroin –Commercially produced by Bayer until 1898 and afterwards for medicinal purposes and as a "non-addictive" substitute for morphine addiction. Not banned in U. S. until 1924.

---

[40] "Ten Illegal Drugs That Used to be Sold Over-the-Counter", Business Pundit, <http://www.business
Pundit.com/10-illegal-drugs-that-used-to-be-sold over> 27 April 2013

Up until about the time of Prohibition, those who developed a dependency on narcotics were looked upon as having a medical problem, not as criminals, and were treated accordingly without fanfare or manufacturing a national crime problem.

As late as 1916, the Supreme Court, led by Chief Justice Oliver Wendell Holmes by a vote of 7-2 threw out an indictment against a Pittsburgh physician for writing a narcotics prescription for an addict.[41]

Passage of the Harrison Act in 1914 inadvertently spelled the end of long standing common sense traditions regarding drugs. The Harrison Act was intended to insure the orderly distribution of narcotics, primarily opium and cocaine (coca leaves). Being a physician was no longer sufficient to legally prescribe narcotics. They now had to obtain a special license at a moderate fee to do so. [42]

Unfortunately, the Law of Unintended Consequences reared its ugly head. A clause in the law stated, "Nothing contained in this section shall apply…to the dispensing or distribution of any of the aforesaid drugs to a patient by a physician… registered under this Act *in the course of his professional practice only"*. Police officers began to interpret the clause "in the course of his professional practice only" to mean that a doctor could not prescribe maintenance levels of opiates to an addict because, in the thought processes of law enforcement, addiction was not an illness. Therefore an addict could not be considered a patient and supplied with narcotics even if prescribed or dispensed by a physician properly licensed. To do so was construed as a violation of the Harrison Act. Many physicians in fact were subsequently arrested and imprisoned. [43]

From that point forward, opium and cocaine could no longer be obtained through legitimate medical channels. Consequently, as legal avenues dried up, illicit sources opened

---

[41] Mike Gray "Drug Crazy:", p. 56
[42] Elaine Casey, "History of Drug Use and Drug Users"
[43] Ibid.

up to supply users. The Supreme Court ruled in the early 1920s that prescriptions for addicts did not constitute the practice of medicine. That ruling made addiction a federal crime. As a result, addicts were forced to seek their medication from the underground Black Market controlled by mob bosses and street gangs, thereby triggering the first significant entrée into narcotics trafficking.[44]

In 1920, sale of alcohol was banned under the law that came to be known as Prohibition. Public pressure led to its repeal in 1933 under the sponsorship of the Roosevelt administration. It did nothing to stop consumption of alcohol, but it did create organized crime in this country, another example of the Law of Unintended Consequences.

If we ask, "who benefitted from Prohibition", the answer would be those who were opposed to the sale of alcohol and those who supplied it illegally. It is one of those ironies of life that people who favor prohibiting a particular indulgence become the unwitting bed partner of the criminal elements who will provide the prohibited indulgence. It should cause the morally upright some discomfort that their interests are not only aligned with their mortal enemy, they are aiding and abetting them in creating a profitable criminal enterprise and helping spawn violent crimes that inflict far worse damage on society than the very behavior they are trying to prohibit.

When Prohibition was finally repealed in 1933, the criminal elements went out of the alcohol distribution business because the public sale and consumption of alcohol became legal, meaning it was regulated and taxed. There was no longer a need for a Black Market. The liquor store and corner bar replaced the bootlegger and mobster. Violent crime eventually subsided to pre-Prohibition levels.

At the end of the day, society was better off allowing people to indulge their particular craving rather than prohibiting it. No matter how much one may have considered alcohol

---

[44] Ibid.

consumption to be a moral blight needing to be corrected, the human misery created by Prohibition was exponentially greater than the ill effects of people indulging in drinking.

CHAPTER THREE

Declaration of War on Drugs[45]

In 1971, angered by marijuana smoking, anti-war hippies, Richard Nixon declared War on Drugs. Congress passed the Comprehensive Drug Abuse Prevention and Control Act which established the national Commission on Marijuana and Drug Abuse.

Intending for the Commission to find a scientific basis for justifying the administration's hard line approach to marijuana, Nixon appointed as Chairman of the Commission, Ray Shafer, a former Pennsylvania governor known to be an avid anti-drug Republican. Nixon also appointed to the Commission the dean of a law school, a retired Chicago police captain, two senators and two congressmen equally divided between each party, and four doctors, including the head of a mental health hospital. Nixon made clear to Shafer that the Commission's final report should come out conclusively against marijuana.

After months of study, which involved reviewing numerous research projects on the effects of marijuana and interviewing medical experts, the commission's final report contained some surprising conclusions and recommendations. Remember this was almost four decades ago. The report exposed a number of the myths and misconceptions about marijuana. One of its conclusions was "marijuana's relative potential for harm to the vast majority of individual users and its actual impact on society does not justify a social policy designed to seek out and firmly punish those who use it".

The Commission could find no medical evidence that marijuana served as a gateway to the use of harder drugs and

---

[45] "1960s, The Hippy Trail, and Nixon"
<http://www.hempnowbook.com/1960s-the-hippy-trail-and-Nixon.html> 21 April, 2010

determined that alcohol was a greater risk than marijuana. They recommended the personal use of marijuana should be decriminalized, as should selling or exchanging small amounts:

> "..marijuana use is not such a grave problem that individuals who smoke marijuana, or possess it for that purpose, should be subject to criminal procedures".

The Commission found that the constitutionality of marijuana prohibition was suspect and that the executive and legislative branches had a duty to obey the Constitution, even in the absence of a court ruling to do so. It also recommended removing any distinctions between licit and illicit drugs:[46]

> "...the use of drugs for pleasure or other non-medical purposes is not inherently irresponsible; alcohol is widely used as an acceptable part of social activities"

The Shafer Commission Report was endorsed by the American Medical Association, The American Bar Association, The American Public Health Association, The National Education Association and The National Council of Churches. An angry Nixon tossed the study into the trash without even reading it.

Political conservatives like George Schultz, William Buckley and Milton Friedman began expressing concern with the hypocrisy of the nation's drug laws. By the time Jimmy Carter became President, eleven states had reduced the offense of marijuana possession to the equivalent of receiving a traffic ticket.[47]

---

[46] National Commission on Marihuana and Drug Abuse, <http://wikipedia.org/wiki/National_Commision_ on_Marihuana-and_Drug_Abuse> 21 April 2010
[47] Mike Gray, "Drug Crazy", p. 98

Carter, a born-again Christian, favored the decriminalization of marijuana.[48] In 1977, President Carter's Drug Czar, an ex-Army Captain and respected Stanford trained psychiatrist named Peter Bourne, repeated the recommendation of the Shafer commission calling for elimination of penalties for marijuana possession. Unfortunately, Dr. Bourne became embroiled in a controversy and resigned. It was discovered that he had written a prescription for Quaaludes for one of his staffers. [49]Carter faced other political crises and the recommendation to remove the penalties for use of marijuana fell through the cracks.

---

[48] Ibid, p. 98
[49] "Peter Bourne", <http://en.wikipedia.org/wiki/Peter_Bourne> 28 April 2013

CHAPTER FOUR

Flawed Premises of the Drug War

The War on Drugs is based on a number of flawed premises.

The first flawed premise is that we must outlaw drugs because all drugs are harmful, that everyone who uses drugs becomes addicted and addicts commit violent crimes either to support their habit or because they have lost control of their mental faculties.

None of the above is even remotely correct.

This premise is not only simplistic, it misleads the public into "being tough" unnecessarily on drug users. Like many premises, there is an element of truth in this one. People can be out of control or commit crimes to fund their addiction. However, the notion that there are thousands of potheads, heroin and coke addicts running amuck holding up convenience stores and committing violent crimes is patently untrue. The overwhelming majority of drug offenders have never committed a violent crime in their life. Most are guilty only of simple possession. The Department of Justice Report on Alcohol and Crime and the National Institute of Health found that alcohol is more often associated with both violent and nonviolent crime than illicit drugs such as marijuana and heroin.[50]

The violent crime associated with drugs comes primarily from drug suppliers seeking to protect or expand their profits by engaging in turf battles over territorial distribution rights or to intimidate law enforcement and local citizenry through acts of terror. Let's not forget Prohibition. The homicide rate almost doubled during Prohibition and returned to normal after its repeal. Neither the increase or decrease in crime had anything to do with the people who were drinking. The decrease resulted

---

[50] "Drug Use and violent crimes among adolescents", Adolescence, 1997 Summer; 32(126):395-405,
   <http://www.ncbi.nlm.nih.gov/pubmed/9179335>   5 May 2013

from removing the profits from alcohol trafficking by making consumption of alcohol legal then regulating and taxing it.

Much of what we have been told, and therefore believe, about drugs is based on archaic and prejudicial beliefs that have been proven to be incorrect or simply misconceptions. For example, the belief that people cannot use drugs recreationally, that is without becoming addicted, is pure nonsense. Yet, it's a commonly held belief. The vast majority of people who use drugs are recreational users. A recreational drug user is the equivalent of a social drinker. They can use the drug of their choice, including heroin or cocaine, and still be functioning, responsible people who hold jobs, attend church and be otherwise respectable upstanding citizens.

There is absolutely, unequivocally no scientific basis that people cannot use drugs recreationally just as they can alcohol. It is estimated that approximately 200 million people worldwide use drugs at least once a year and another 110 million use drugs on a monthly basis. Those 310 million individuals are considered to be recreational drugs users, while the 25 million who use drugs more frequently are considered to be drug abusers. [51]Indeed, as we will see shortly, two of the most addictive substances in the world are cigarettes and alcohol and they are infinitely more harmful and result in far more deaths than any illicit drug. In fact, nicotine is the most addictive and deadliest substance we could ingest.

As the Shafer Commission noted, marijuana is a harmless substance unless laced with impurities or a more powerful drug such as PCP. In recorded history there has never been one death attributable to marijuana. Unlike harder drugs, it is impossible to overdose on marijuana and addiction is rare.[52] In fact, marijuana

---

[51] Recreational Drug Use,
<http://www.quotes.orthodoxwiki.org/Recreational_drug_use> 22 April 2010
[52] Nicolas Morine, "The War on Drugs, Truly A War on People – Misguided Stigma Attached to Pot
Smoking Still Alive and Well:", December 22, 2008 <http://international-human-rughts.suite101,com/

is a safer substance than alcohol, tobacco, prescription medications and even aspirin. While no one has ever died from using marijuana, approximately 17,000 people die each year from using aspirin and over the counter aspirin-like substances (non-steroidal anti-inflammatory drugs) such as Ibuprofen and Naproxen. [53]

Virtually every reputable medical organization, such as the prestigious National Institute of Medicine, has echoed the Schafer Commission's findings about marijuana. The Institute of Medicine also discounts fears that use of marijuana serves as a "gateway" to harder drug use. A study conducted ten years ago by the Institute reported:

> "…because underage smoking and alcohol use typically precede marijuana use, marijuana is not the most common, and is rarely the first 'gateway' to illicit drugs". There is no conclusive evidence that the drug effects of marijuana are casually linked to the subsequent use of other illicit drugs". [54]

In short, we have criminalized one group of mood altering substances while legalizing others that are substantially more addictive and harmful, and spent a trillion dollars defending such an absurd policy.

The second flawed premise is that the best way to deter demand is to outlaw drugs and punish people who use them. And punish them we have. According to the FBI's Uniform Crime

---

article,cfm/the_war_in_drugs_truly_a_war_> 7 April 2010
[53] Annual Causes of Death in the United States
<http://www.drugwarfacts.org/cms/?q=node/30>,
    27 April, 2013
[54] "Marijuana and Medicine: Assessing the Science Base", Institute of Medicine, Janet E. Joy,
    Stanley J. Watson, Jr. and John A. Benson, editors, National Academy Press, 1Washington, D. C.,
    1999 <http://www.duglibrary.org/schaffer/library/studies/iom/iom0.htm> 5 May 2913

Report, we have arrested over 40 million individuals for drug related offenses in the last 40 years. Roughly half of all those arrests were for marijuana and over 40% were for simple possession of marijuana.[55] Over the past ten years, we have arrested on average over 700,000 people a year for simple possession of marijuana. Basically, we are arresting each year almost one million people whose only crime is using a safer, healthier substance than alcohol, tobacco, prescription pharmaceuticals, or even aspirin. [56]

Incarcerations for drug offenses have quadrupled since 1980. [57] The United States now has over two million of its citizens incarcerated, a seven fold increase over 1980 levels and more than any other nation in the world. [58] According to the Bureau of Prisons, the single greatest reason for the growth in the prison population has been the war on drugs.[59]

So bent are we on punishing non-violent drug offenders, the average sentence for a drug offender has almost doubled, from 47 months to 82 months while the average sentence in federal courts for violent crimes decreased from 125 months to 88 months. In other words, being caught with drugs merited about the same sentence as killing someone. [60]

Short of making drug possession a capital offense, it's hard to imagine how it would be possible to be more punitive in our treatment of drug violators than we have been. Yet, demand

---

[55] "Drug War Facts", 25 April, 2013
[56] "The War on Drugs, Truly a War on People", December 22, 2008
<http://international-human-rights.
    suite101.com/article.cfm/the_war_on_drugs_truly_a_war_> 7 April, 2010
[57] "Incarceration in the United States"
<http://en.wikipedia.org/wiki/Incarceration_in_the_United_States>
    22 April, 2010
[58] Ibid
[59] Ibid
[60] Randall G. Shelden, "The Prison-Industrial Complex",
<http://www.populist.com/99.11.prison.html>
    3 May, 2010

for drugs is greater than ever and drugs are more plentiful than ever.

The third flawed premise is that another avenue for stopping drug use is to cut off their availability, or supply. By toppling drug lords and dealers, dismantling their organizations and destroying drugs at their source or intercepting them before they enter the country, we would put the traffickers out of business or at least put a major dent in their profits. How we could forget the farce of alcohol prohibition, which was based on the exact same premise with exactly the same futile outcome. It didn't work then and it isn't working now. We have a 40 year history and a trillion dollars spent to prove that approach is never going to work.

For every drug kingpin or dealer removed, there are a hundred wannabes waiting to take their place. For every field of poppies we have destroyed, ten more are blooming in a new locale. And we've already shown that interdiction flat out does not work.

When Pablo Escobar was gunned down while fleeing barefoot across a Columbian barrio rooftop, excited DEA agents put a red X over a flyer with his picture on it. His was one of sixteen such flyers of major drug lords. Agents felt if they could simply X out the other fifteen, the Drug War would be won. Eventually the faces of all sixteen were marked out by a big red X. Did ridding the planet of the top 16 major drug traffickers cripple drug trafficking or inflict even a nominal wound to their organizations? No, nothing changed.[61] Despite all the measures we took, traffickers outsmarted us and drugs continue to flow in an unstoppable current.

The Black Market is ruled by the law of the jungle: the survival of the fittest. The drug traffickers adapted. The whole structure of the supply chain changed. The old school of drug warlords was succeeded by a new generation of younger, smarter but more ruthless and violent criminal masterminds. In one

---

[61] Wallace-Wells, "How American Lost the War on Drugs"

Mexican town, drug cartels promised to kill a police officer every 48 hours until the local sheriff resigned. After two police officers were murdered, he stepped down. In some cities, cartels have threatened to attack elementary school buses. [62]

Cartels merged to eliminate the risks and costs of competing with one another and to assure mutual survival. Smaller cartels, more nimble and more hi-tech arose. Drug crime shifted from domestic, regional traffickers to global trafficking that is transnational in nature and increasingly networked with other criminal groups. [63] The globalization of finance, trade and high-tech communications made the trafficking process easier to carry out and harder for law enforcement to control.[64] Drug distribution moved from Columbia to Mexico. In Juarez, a mid level cocaine trafficker named Amado Fuentes created a new style of cartel that was based on the business model used by legitimate corporations. He brought in management professionals such as lawyers, accountants, human resource and information system specialists. He even created an acquisitions division. Before long, Fuentes had a fleet of 727s for transporting up to fifteen tons of cocaine at a time [65]

The outcome of our military style crackdown on drugs has been a series of unintended consequences that have only made things worse. Vincente Fox, the former president of Mexico, tried to clean up the corruption left by the prior administration. He fired tens of thousands of dirty cops. In cleaning up corruption in the military, ninety thousand soldiers from the Mexican army were either fired or deserted. Many of

---

[62] Patrick Cooley, "The Mexican Drug War and How it Affects the United States", April 13, 2009,
  <http://internationalaffairs.suite101.com/article.cfm/the_mexican_drug_war > 7 April, 2010
[63] :Drug War Facts", <http://www/drugwarfacts.org/cms/Crime> 25 April 2012
[64] "Drug Trafficking", Wise to Social Issues,
<http://socialissues.wiseto.com/Articles/FO3020640073/>
  25 April, 2010
[65] Wallace-Wells, "How America Lost the War on Drugs"

22

the fired police and terminated soldiers were then recruited by drug lords, effectively increasing their combat muscle and professionalizing their fighting capabilities.[66]

The end result of our efforts to dismantle the drug cartels has been to transform them into transnational organizations. With the global expansion of drug trafficking cartels are now establishing distinct cells in cities throughout the world, including the United States. [67]

We tried destroying drugs at their source. We paid farmers not to grow cocoa leaves. We sprayed cocoa fields with poisonous chemicals. [68] Cocoa crops moved to Bolivia and Peru. [69] New meth labs popped up faster than we could shut them down. The number of clandestine amphetamine labs is reported to have increased 20% in 2008, many in countries where such labs had never before been detected. [70] Asian poppy fields offset loss of poppy production in Afghanistan. Basically, the world is simply too large to police. When faced with initiatives to destroy or limit their production, traffickers have consistently found new cultivation areas, new transit zones and new markets. [71]

The Government Accounting Office ("GAO") reported that the U. S. government's $6 billion investment in wiping out Columbia's coca crops and cocaine production had been a failure. [72] Known as Plan Columbia, the aid program was aimed at shrinking coca and cocaine supply. Instead, coca production

---

[66] Wallace-Wells, "How America Lost the War on Drugs"

[67] "Mexican Drug Trafficking Organizations", DrugWarFacts.org, <http://www.drugwarfacts.org/cms/
    Crime> 25 April, 2013

[68] "Eradication",
<http://stopthedrugwar.org/topics/drug_war_issues/criminal_justice/policing/e
radi-
    cation?page=5> 29 April, 2013

[69] "War on Drugs" <http://en.wikipedia.org/wiki/War_on_Drugs> 24 April,
2013

[70] "World Drug Report 2010"

[71] "Drug War Facts", 25 April, 2012

[72] "Eradication"

was up 15% and cocaine production was up 4%. [73] And the wellspring of drugs continued to flood our country.

The fourth flawed premise is treating acts that are harmful only to the person committing them as criminal offenses. A fundamental principle of the law is if there is no victim, there is no crime. Even if drug use was a proven health hazard, people indulging in drugs would be guilty of inflicting harm only on themselves, no different than people who over eat, don't exercise, smoke and drink. In this sense, they are both the "perpetrator" and the "victim". However, unlike other criminal statutes, drug laws provide no justice for the "victim". The person who has "victimized" themselves through self-inflicted abuse is one-sidedly convicted as a criminal while their status as a victim is disregarded. The law could just as easily have protected the "victim" side of the offense. This schizophrenic approach is contrary to the historic mission of government which is to protect us from one another, not from ourselves.

---

[73] Ibid

CHAPTER FIVE

Use Rates
Illicit Drugs, Alcohol and Tobacco

Each year, the Substance Abuse and Mental Health Services Administration of the department of Health and Human Services conducts the National Survey on Drug Use and Health (NSDUH). The Office of Applied Statistics (OAS), part of SAMHSA, publishes the results of these surveys on line at www.oas.samhsa.gov/facts.cfm. The survey breaks down frequency of use by three categories: The number of people aged 12 or older reporting any drug use over their lifetime; the number of people 12 and older reporting any drug use over the past twelve months and the number reporting any drug use in the prior month. This latter category is also called "Current Users" under the presumption that someone who reported using drugs in the past month is probably more of a repeat user.

In terms of the numbers of people who reported using various substances in the 2010 survey during the previous twelve months and in the month previous to the survey, here is the breakdown by drug use at age 12 or older. The top half of the table lists drugs that are illegal to use. The bottom half list substances that are not necessarily illegal, but are the most "abused" form of medications or other substances that can be obtained legally:

Table I

2010
Drug Use Past Year and Past Month
Ages 12 and Older

Illicit Drug	Users Past Year	Users Past Month
Marijuana	29,206,000	17,373,000
Cocaine	4,499,000	1,466,000
Crack	871,000	378,000
Heroin	618,000	239,000
Hallucinogens	4,517,000	1,208,000
LSD	874,000	154,000
PCP	95,000	35,000
Ecstasy	2,645,000	695,000
Total Illicit Drug Users	36,776,000	21,937,000

Legal Substances:	Abusers Past Year	Abusers Past Month
Inhalants	2,030,000	685,000
Non-medical use of		
Psychotherapeutics	16,031,000	6,967,000
Pain Relievers	12,213,000	5,100,000
OxyContin	1,869,000	564,000
Tranquilizers	5,581,000	2,160,000
Stimulants	2,887,000	1,077,000
Methamphetamines	934,000	374,000
Sedatives	811,000	374,000
Sub-Total: Abusers of Legal Substances	18,061,000	7,652,000
Grand Total	54,837,000	28,747,000

NOTE: Some of the drugs listed above are sub-categories of other drugs and are shown indented under their parent category.

26

Approximately 22 million people were current users of illegal drugs. Of that number, about 17 million used primarily marijuana and the remaining 4.6 million used what might be termed "harder" drugs that are addictive and more lethal. In other words, around 80% of illicit drug use in this country relates to consumption of marijuana, a product that virtually every reputable medical source in the world has repeatedly said is non-addictive and harmless. Not one death has ever been linked to use of marijuana. Virtually every study commissioned by the government recommends decriminalizing it.

The remaining 4.6 million people who used harder drugs represent roughly 1.5% of the population of the United States. Think about the implications of these numbers. It means we have spent trillions of dollars and imprisoned millions of people in an effort to stop 1.5% of the population from indulging in drugs. As a matter of public policy how insane is that?

The percentage of the population that abuse legal drugs is almost double the number who engage in hard drug use. How much money have we spent on that problem? How many of those people have we arrested and imprisoned? As one example, Inhalants represent close to one thousand ordinary household products that can be legally purchased from any local hardware store or supermarket such as such as paint, turpentine, glue, lighter fluid, hair sprays, magic markers, air fresheners, gasoline and vegetable cooking sprays. More people used Inhalants (685,000) than used Crack Cocaine and Heroin combined (467,000). Why haven't we declared War on Inhalants?

What the information in Table I shows is that we are criminalizing and spending prohibitive sums of money to prevent access to some forms of substance use but allowing access by a greater number of people to other substances that are legal, even though the legal substance is being abused and kills more people than the illegal substances.

Table II

2010
Drug, Alcohol & Tobacco Use
Ages 12 and Older

Substance:	Users Past Year	Users Past Month
Illicit Drug users	36,766.000	21,937,000
Total tobacco users:	83,200,000	69,559,000
Cigarettes	68,458,000	58,256,000
Smokeless tobacco	12,334,000	8,855,000
Cigars	25,833,000	13,177,000
Pipes	(Not collected)	2,150,000
Total drinkers:	168,396,000	131,342,000
Binge drinkers	n/a	58,550,000
Heavy drinkers	n/a	16,931,000

Table III

2010
Percentage of U.S. Population Substance Usage – Past Month
(Aged 12 or Older)

Category	Total %	Total % Excluding Marijuana
Illegal Drug Use	9.1%	1.5%
Cigarettes	23.6%	23.6%
Alcohol	53.2%	53.2%
Heavy Drinkers	6.9%	6.9%

NOTE: The U. S. Census in 2010 was 308,747,508. Approximately 80% were older than 14, or about 247 million. That number was the cohort used to calculate the above percentages.

Table III shows the magnitude of use of substances that the majority of medical and law enforcement sources would classify as "harmful" to the user.

These numbers help explain the astounding disparity between the number of people who die from using illegal drugs versus alcohol and tobacco. Approximately 435,000 people die annually from smoking, about 110,000 die from the effects of drinking but only about 17,000 people die from the effects of illegal drug use. [74]

In short, (i) illicit drugs are less lethal and addictive than alcohol and nicotine, (ii) no one has ever died from smoking marijuana, (iii) the "violence" associated with illicit drug use is due to ruthless drug cartels who are wreaking havoc on our justice system, funding international terrorism and destabilizing national governments. These cartels would not exist if drugs now outlawed were legalized. So why are we ruining the lives of young men and women and why are we spending $40 to $50 billion of dollars each year in a futile effort that serves no justifiable purpose and has achieved no worthwhile result?

The SAMHSA Survey does not enumerate the percentage of illegal drug users who are "addicts". However, based on past governmental surveys and research conducted by various health organizations, it is estimated that there are approximately 310 million people in the world who use illegal drugs and about 25 million are abusers, or roughly 8%. [75] Based on 21.9 million Current Users, that would mean there are approximately 1.75 million people in the United States addicted to illegal drugs. If we assume that 90% of Current smokers are addicted to nicotine, that would equal about 52 million people and would represent 30 times more people addicted to cigarettes than illicit drugs. The

---

[74] "Annual Causes of Death in the United States",<
http://www.drugfacts.org/cms/?Q=node/30>
27 April, 2013
[75] "Recreational Drug Use"
<http://www.quotes,.orthodoxwiki.org/Recreational_drug_use> 22 April 2010

number of "heavy drinkers" (i.e., virtual alcoholics) at 16.9 million is almost ten times the number of people addicted to drugs.

The inconsistency of warring on drugs while closing our eyes to the greater health damage inflicted by addictive legal substances was noted by the former Surgeon General of the United States, Everett Koop in testifying at a U. S. Trade Representation panel:

> "...when we are pleading with foreign governments to stop the flow of cocaine, it is the height of hypocrisy for the U. S. to export tobacco. Years from now, we will look back on this application of free trade policy and find it scandalous". [76]

Someone once said that "useless laws weaken necessary laws". More people are beginning to understand that alcohol and nicotine (and a number of prescription medications) are mood altering substances just as illicit drugs are and that each of those substances are more addictive and more harmful than any illicit drug, marijuana in particular.

As the War on Drugs has shown, people who use drugs are not going to stop taking them because they know better than anyone that drugs are not the menace they have been portrayed for so many years. That belief is increasingly being shared by society in general, virtually all medical organizations and by mounting numbers of the justice and law enforcement communities who realize the illogic of prohibiting "some" mood altering substances that are less dangerous than those that are legal.

The opposition to drug prohibition continues to grow as people have become educated about drugs and can see first hand

---

[76] Everett Koop testimony before U. S. Trade Representative panel, 1989
<http://libcom.org/history/
    Articles/war-on-drugs> 8 May 2013

that much of the propaganda over the past decades has been misguided, erroneous or deliberately misrepresented.

The factual data indicates that the War on Drugs has been misleading the American people and perpetrating myths about the so-called "dangers" of drugs, rather than telling them the truth, primarily to justify a hard stance on crime for political purposes.

Dr. Joseph McNamara, a veteran of the New York City Police Department and a former Chief of Police of both Kansas City and San Jose acknowledges that the Drug War is politically motivated and that politicians are afraid to confront the reality of the need for reform. He believes that like Vietnam, the Drug War could not stand the light of day if the American people had all the facts. They would quickly realize that the vast majority of professional law enforcement officials feel the War on Drugs is a politically motivated propaganda campaign designed to help politicians win votes by being viewed as "tough on crime" and to justify pouring billions of tax dollars into the criminal justice system. [77]

Americans pride themselves on their rugged individualism and generally resist to the extent possible government interference in their personal lives. Yet, in being "tough on crime", even the rugged individualists have acquiesced to government intrusion into a person's rights to personal freedom. As a result, the Law of Unintended Consequences kicked in and the "cure" turned out to be a bigger and costlier problem than the illness.

Aside from being a flawed plan from the outset and a monumental failure in its execution, the most sobering consequence of the War on Drugs is the collateral damage it has inflicted both at home and across the globe.

---

[77] Hoover Law Enforcement Summit, may 17, 1995
<http://www.mapinc.org/alert/0158.html>
   7 May 2013

CHAPTER SIX

Collateral Damage of Drug War

Exploding Prison Population and Exponential Growth of the Justice System

While a dubious distinction, no other society in human history has ever imprisoned so many of its own citizens for purposes of crime control than the United States. [78]

If the criminal justice system were a public company, its stock price would be growing through the roof. Total combined expenditures for the various components of the justice system (police, courts and prisons) increased by more than 400% between 1982-2003 and are estimated to be approximately $215 billion annually. [79]

Largely as the result of the drug war, and electing imprisonment over fines, community service or treatment, the United States now has the distinction of having both the highest known incarceration rate in the world and the highest number of its citizens behind bars. In 2008, there were 2.3 million inmates in the United States, or four times the number of inmates in 1982. Approximately 1.5 million were in federal and state prisons, 748,000 were in local jails and the rest were in juvenile facilities, military or territorial facilities. It is estimated that approximately one million of the total incarcerated population are serving time for non-violent offenses. [80]

Until the 1970s, when the War on Drugs was launched, for most of the 20th century the rate of incarceration in this

---

[78] Schlosser
[79] "Economics-Statistics-United States", DrugWarFacts.org
<http://drugwarfacts.org/cms?q=node/38> ,
    9 April, 2010
[80] "Incarceration", Wikipedia
<http://en.wikipedia.org/wiki/incarceration_in_the_United_States>
    22 April 2010

32

country held steady at about 110 inmates per 100,000 population. At the end of 2008, the rate was 754 inmates per 100,000 population, almost seven times the rate at the beginning of the drug war and 6 to 10 times higher than most Western nations who consume illicit drugs at about the same rate per capita as Americans but which have significantly lower crime rates.[81] Our incarceration rate is eight times that of Germany whose rate is 93 per 100,000 population. Our rate is also higher than nations that we think of as having oppressive regimes such as Russia, China and Rawanda. With four times the population, and a much less tolerant government, Communist China has about 1.5 million people serving time, or 800,000 less than we do. In terms of incarceration rate, Russia is second with a rate of 638 inmates per 100,000 population, 18% lower than the U. S.[82] Rawanda's incarceration rate is 565 per 100,000.[83]

As the greatest democracy in the free world, and one known for its commitment to human rights, it seems paradoxical and a contradiction with our nation's historical values, that the United States ranks above two totalitarian regimes in terms of the frequency by which it imprisons non-violent citizens.

The explosion in our prison population is due almost exclusively to one variable: drug related arrests. According to the most current FBI report, in 2011 there were approximately 12.4 million arrests. The most frequent cause was drug abuse violations, estimated by the FBI at 1.5 million.[84] In 2007 872,720 people were arrested for marijuana related offenses. Of that number, 775,137 were for simple possession.

---

[81] Ibid
[82] Drug War Facts, "Global Prison Population Rates"
[83] Drug War Facts, "Prisons, Jails and Probation"
<http://www.drugwarfacts.org/cms/?q=node/62>,,
    27 April, 2013
[84] "2011 Crime Report", United States Department of Justice, Federal Bureau of Investigation, Uniform
    Crime Report, Justice Information Services Division

The cost of this level of incarceration is staggering. It costs about $70 a day or around $25,500 a year to keep an adult in state or federal prison.[85] With our current jail and prison population, we are now spending about $165 million *per day* and $60 billion per year just to incarcerate individuals.[86]

To pursue a policy of punishment while ignoring treatment is like locking the barn door after the horse has already escaped. The shortsightedness of a punitive approach was confirmed by a study prepared by the Rand Corporation, a conservative think tank group. The study revealed that drug treatment is seven times more cost-effective than arresting people and ten times more effective than keeping drugs from entering the country. [87]

Even China has come to recognize the need to shift away from a purely punitive model. In 2008, it adopted a new policy, a Drug Control Law, as part of a reform movement where drug addiction is no longer a legal or moral issue, but a complicated medical condition requiring comprehensive therapeutic treatment.[88]

As we bemoan the problems in our educational systems, the War on Drugs is making a growth industry out of the prison system. As already stated, about 1,000 new prisons and jails have been built over the past several decades primarily to accommodate the exponential growth in the inmate population

---

[85] "Correction Systems Cost Per Offender", Drug War Facts, Prisons, Jails and Probation, <http://www. Drugwarfacts.org/cms?q=node 62> 27 April 2013
[86] Ibid
[87] "Economic Consequences of the War on Drugs", Drug Policy Alliance, 2002, <http://www.drugpol-icy.org/library/factsheets/economiccons/fact_economic.cfm> 9 April, 2010
[88] "Looking for a solution for drug addition in China", Drug Policy, Volume 21, Issue 3, pages 149-154 , (May, 2010) <http://www.ijdp.org/article/SO955-3595%/2809%2099128-5/abstract>, 24 April, 2010

who are drug offenders. Given that the cost per bed of prison and jail construction ranges from $50,000 to $200,000 or more, it is estimated that that the cost of that expansion was in the vicinity of $50 billion to $100 billion. [89]

In another parallel to the War on Drugs, prison populations swelled during Prohibition. Prior to 1920, there were approximately 4,000 federal convicts. By 1932, the year before repeal, the number of federal convicts had increased to over 10,000, or 250%. In 1930, over two-thirds of prisoners had been convicted on alcohol and drug related charges. [90] According to Mike Gray:

> "In the first year of Prohibition, crime leaped 25% in the nation's major cities, and before the decade was over the criminal justice system would be overwhelmed. The federal caseload tripled and civil cases were brushed aside to make room for the flood of alcohol offenders…The federal prison system was operating at 170% capacity and the cost to the taxpayers was about to increased by an order of magnitude".[91]

Contributing to the exploding inmate population is the impact of mandatory sentencing laws that can make punishment for a first time drug offense worse than for violent crimes. Under mandatory sentencing guidelines car thieves, killers, sexual abusers and robbers can receive lighter prison sentences than a person convicted of possessing marijuana or five grams of cocaine.

We need to recall the Law of Unintended Consequences. Ostensibly directed at putting drug lords and drug dealers behind bars, mandatory sentencing has caught in its web, non-violent

[89] "The Real Costs of Prison Construction", Prison Construction, <http://www.realcostofprison>
[90] "Crime Rate", <http://library.thinkquest.org/04oct/00492/Crime_Rate.htm> 22 April,. 2010
[91] Mike Gray, "Drug Crazy", p. 67

run-of-the-mill drug users or even ordinary people caught in questionable circumstances. Kentucky Justice Secretary J. Michael Brown said in testimony to the state of Kentucky Senate Judiciary Committee in January, 2008:

> "I don't think we're getting the worst drug lords into the prisons. We're just getting the people who went out and got caught. It's the low hanging fruit".[92]

The failure of our punitive approach to drugs echoes the failure of Prohibition in eliminating alcohol. Mike Gray, author of *The China Syndrome*, notes this comparison to Prohibition in his book, *Drug Crazy:*

> "Confronted with the ongoing failure of law enforcement, the prohibitionists demanded more of it – tougher judges, harsher penalties, more draconian punishment. By 1929, the penalties had been ratcheted up by a factor of ten. You could now get five years and a $10,000 fine for selling one drink. The enforcement budget was tripled, more agents hired, the Fourth Amendment was practically set aside". [93]

Being "tough on crime" can actually create more crime than it prevents. The murder rate in the U. S. soared after enactment of Prohibition in 1920 from about 5.6 murders per 100,000 to almost 10 murders per 100,000, a 78% increase over pre-prohibition America. When Prohibition ended in 1933, the rate began dropping like a rock and by 1940 stood at 6 murders per 100,000. [94]

And the effect of stepping up penalties and imprisonment? Reports Gray, "and still it (alcohol) came in, an unstoppable wellspring of booze flowing from breweries in

---

[92] "One in 100 Behind Bars", Pew Center on the States and the Public Safety Performance Project, p. 7,
    <www.pewcenteronthestates.org> , 7 April, 2010
[93] Mike Gray, "Drug Crazy", p. 69
[94] "Crime Rate", 22 April, 2010

basements, and from breweries that covered acres operating at full tilt with the complete cooperation of local officials, and from three hundred thousand private stills spread all over the country". [95]

Corruption

Just as Prohibition led to wide spread corruption among law enforcement agencies and our justice system, so has the War on Drugs sparked the exact same phenomenon and for precisely the same reasons – enormous amounts of money.

A 1998 report by the General Accounting Office ("GAO") of the United States government disclosed drug-related police corruption in Atlanta, Chicago, Cleveland, Detroit, Los Angeles, Miami, New Orleans, Philadelphia, Washington, D. C. and Savannah. The GAO reported that from 1993-1998, the FBI opened at least 400 state and local police corruption cases that were drug-related, leading to the conviction of over 300 officers. [96]

Below is a random list of examples of drug-related corruption cases within law enforcement departments:

- Florida
    - February, 2001. Three South Florida police officers were indicted for drug trafficking, including using patrol cars to transport drug dealers.
    - October, 2001. Two current and former Hialeah police officers were charged with protecting and assisting drug dealers and serving as lookouts.
    - Late 1980s. More than 100 Miami Police Department officers were arrested, suspended or

---

[95] Mike Gray, "Drug Crazy", p. 69
[96] "Police Corruption", <u>Drug Policy & The Law</u>, <http:www.drugpolicy.org/law/police/ > 19 April, 2010

punished in a series of drug-related corruption cases. [97]

- Los Angeles:
  - 2000-2001. One of the nation's worst incidents of police corruption was the "Rampart Scandal". Over one hundred drug convictions were overturned as the result of revelations of misconduct by police officers, including planting evidence, confessions obtained through beatings, framing innocent people, torture, drug dealing and even murder. [98]

- Illinois
  - 2000. Two veteran police officers from an elite drug-fighting unit were arrested for robbery, corruption, planting evidence and running a Chicago to Miami drug ring. The officers were also indicted for tipping off other dealers to the identities of informants and undercover police officers.
  - 1997. Three tactical officers of Chicago's 6th District were arrested for conspiracy to commit robbery and sales of illegally confiscated narcotics.[99]

- North Carolina
  - 2001. Four county narcotics officers were charged in a federal indictment with conspiracy to distribute cocaine, marijuana, Ecstasy and steroids.[100]

---

[97] "Police, Drugs and Corruption", <u>Drug Policy Alliance,</u> <www.drugpolicy.org> 20 April, 2010
[98] Ibid
[99] Ibid
[100] Ibid

- Puerto Rico
  - August, 2001. More than 60 police officers across Puerto Rico were indicted on various drug-related charges, including offering protection services to suspected drug dealers, returning seized drugs to dealers, selling drugs and helping sellers hide during police raids. Twenty nine officers were put behind bars in August, 2001 in what was then the largest police anti-corruption sting in FBI history.
  - January, 2002. Twenty three more officers were arrested. Federal prosecutors charged that prosecutors and judges have acted in collusion with drug traffickers. Two judges were suspended pending an investigation. [101]

- Oakland
  - 2001. Four narcotics officers arrested on misconduct charges. Indicted on 60 counts.[102]

- San Antonio
  - 2001. Eight police officers arrested in a federal sting for plotting to protect a cocaine delivery.[103]

- Cleveland
  - January, 1998. As the result of an FBI undercover operation, 44 police, sheriff's department and corrections officers from 5 law enforcement agencies were charged with taking money to protect cocaine trafficking operations. [104]

---

[101] Ibid
[102] Ibid
[103] Ibid
[104] Ibid

- Detroit
  - 1991. Nine officers charged with conspiracy to aid and abet in the distribution of cocaine and other charges.[105]

- New Orleans
  - 1994. Eleven officers were convicted for protecting a cocaine supply warehouse containing 286 pounds of cocaine.[106]

- Philadelphia
  - Ten policed officers from the 39th District were charged with planting drugs and breaking into homes to steal cash and drugs.[107]

- Savannah
  - Ten officers convicted in 1994 for protecting drug dealers.[108]

- New York
  - Between 1992-1996, thirty officers from Manhattan's 30th precinct were convicted for narcotics-related offenses. In 1992, six officers from Brooklyn precincts were arrested for narcotics crimes stemming from their association with a Suffolk County drug ring.[109]

---

[105] Ibid
[106] Ibid
[107] Ibid
[108] Ibid
[109] Ibid

- Zapata County, TX
    - Most of the county's leaders, including the county sheriff, judge and clerk plead guilty to drug charges. [110]
    -
- U.S. Mexican Border Communities
    - In communities along the border, forty six local, state and federal law enforcement officials have been indicted or convicted on drug charges.[111]

We need to be reminded once again of the parallels to Prohibition. In *Drug Crazy*, Mike Gray documents the corruptive influence of Prohibition:

> By 1929, "…one in four federal agents was dismissed for charges ranging from bribery, extortion, conspiracy and embezzlement to drinking the evidence. In Detroit, the liquor trade was said to be second only to the automobile industry and at a time when hamburgers sold for five cents, payoffs to public officials exceeded two million dollars a week. In New York City the typical speakeasy had to shell out four hundred dollars a month between the Prohibition Bureau, the police department, and the District. Attorney's office, and the lowly beat cop picked up an extra forty dollars every time there was a delivery". [112]

If anyone paid fines and went to jail it was not the guys supplying the booze. It was the ordinary man on the street who wanted to wet his whistle. The organized crime bosses were

---

[110] "The Effective National Drug Control Strategies 1999", <http://www.csdp.org/edcs/page45.htm >,
  19 April, 2010
[111] Ibid
[112] Mike Gray, "Drug Crazy", p. 68

virtually untouchable, due largely to the rampant corruption within the law enforcement community.

During the Johnson Administration the Justice Department noted "evidence of significant corruption" in the Bureau of Narcotics, including buying and selling of drugs and even murder. In 1973, these scandals led Johnson's successor, Richard Nixon, to reorganize federal drug enforcement under a new agency, the DEA. Evidently, the lure of drug money was still too much of a temptation. Within a year of its formation, the DEA was under investigation and the number two man in the agency was forced to resign due to his association with gamblers, felons and drug dealers.[113]

The United States Customs Service, one of the front line defenses on the War of Drugs, monitors more than 300 ports of entry through which illicit drugs flow. Between 2005-2011, a total of 144 employees were arrested or indicted for corruption-related activities, including smuggling of drugs.[114] In one case, in 1990, the Regional Director over San Diego ordered a Customs Inspector and ex-Marine named Mike Horner to turn over the names of his informants. Horner couldn't figure out why the man wanted, or needed this information, but nevertheless, gave it to him since the man was his boss. Four days later one informant was found with a tire iron through his head and a second was stabbed sixteen times and killed.[115] In February 1995, a Customs Inspector working the border at Calexico was booked for "looking the other way" while traffickers brought in six tons of cocaine.[116] A few months later a couple of inspectors in El Paso were charged with helping move twenty-two hundred pounds of cocaine over the border for a slice of the pie worth $1

---

[113] Op Cit. Natural Drug Control Strategy 1999

[114] "Corruption", Drug War Facts, , <http://www.drugwarfacts.org/cms/node/33> 27 April 2013

[115] Mike Gray, "Drug Crazy", p. 147

[116] Ibid, p. 148

million.[117] As Al Capone once said, you don't need to corrupt everybody, just the ones you need, usually a few at the top. [118]

After a while we become numbed to reports of yet another sheriff, policeman, district attorney, judge, customs or federal narcotics agent caught taking bribes from drug dealers or in some cases, selling drugs themselves.

Many professionals in the law enforcement community have become cynical themselves about the drug war, making them even more susceptible to temptation. Every dealer they arrest is quickly replaced by another. At some point, they must think, what's the point? If you can't beat them, why not join up?

As one expert has noted, "The black market is the purest form of unfettered free market capitalism. Rules are Darwinian – survival of the fittest – and no matter what you do, the pirates will always be one step ahead. These are structural forces that like gravity cannot be altered by moral arguments". [119]

Dissembling by the Government

It is difficult to have confidence in a federal policy that the government itself has regularly violated when it suits their purpose. On the one hand, under a policy of prohibition and zero tolerance, teen-aged young men are thrown into prison for four and five years for simple possession while on the other hand, the government freely violates those same laws, by clandestinely dealing in drugs or quietly condones drug trafficking under the guise of national security. In some instances, such as the CIA-Contra scandal, complicity in drug trafficking went to the highest levels of the federal government. By its own admission, the CIA ignored or turned a deaf ear to over 1,000 reports from its field agents of drug trafficking by the Contras. Further, the CIA was

---

[117] Ibid, p. 148
[118] Ibid, p, 148-149
[119] Ibid, p. 188

implicated in financing the purchase of arms with proceeds from cocaine sales. [120]

The War on Drugs has also been used to justify military style operations disguised as a noble cause. Significant amounts of drug war foreign aid money actually goes to right-wing military or para-military groups, who themselves are large-scale narco-traffickers, such as the Colombian military, but who are fighting left-wing insurgents and therefore deemed on the "correct side" of a cause. [121]

In 1989, 25,000 U. S. troops invaded Panama amid much fanfare under the banner of "Operation Just Cause" to remove Panamanian dictator, General Manuel Noriega because of his known involvement in large scale drug trafficking. What was not broadcast was that Noriega had been providing military aid to Contra groups at the request of the U. S. since the 1960s. In return, the U. S. assented to Noriega's continued engagement in drug trafficking. In fact, when the DEA attempted to indict Noriega in 1971, the CIA, under the direction of then CIA director George H. W. Bush, blocked the effort. To add insult to injury, the Bush-led CIA made payments to Noriega of hundreds of thousands of dollars annually for his "work" in Latin America. This fiasco came to an abrupt end when a CIA pilot named Eugene Hasenfus was shot down over Nicaragua by Sandinistas. When documents aboard the plane revealed details of the CIA's activities in Latin America, Noriega became a liability. To avoid a scandal, the government had no choice but to allow the DEA to indict Noriega for drug trafficking after years of condoning his drug operations. Operation Just Cause was launched with much hoopla.[122]

Journalist Gary Webb, in his acclaimed book *Dark Alliance,* detailed how Contras were assisted by the U. S.

---

[120] Op Cit , The Effective National Drug Control Strategy 1999
[121] "War on Drugs", Wikipedia
[122] "U. S. Involvement in Drug Trafficking"
<http://en.wikipedia.org/wiki/War_on_drugs> 24 April 2010

government in distributing crack cocaine into Los Angeles to fund weapons purchases. [123]

The United States sponsored the spraying of lethal chemicals to destroy coca fields in Bolivia and poppy crops in Afghanistan. Unfortunately, the U. S. has not provided any meaningful agricultural alternatives to local farmers whose food crops are destroyed in the process. Worse, the spraying did nothing to eradicate or reduce coca and poppy production. In the six year period 2000-2006, the United States spent $4.7 billion on Plan Colombia for the purpose of eradicating coca production in that nation. The end result? Coca production simply shifted into more remote areas. The overall acreage cultivated for coca in Colombia at the end of the six year period was found to be unchanged. Cultivation in adjacent countries such as Peru and Bolivia actually increased to fill demand.[124] Albert Fujimori, former president of Peru from 1990-2000, described U. S. drug policy as failed. After ten years, and considerable sums of money invested by both Peru and the United States aimed at reducing the supply of coca, the actual supply of coca leaf had actually grown ten fold.[125]

In 2004, Afghan interim president Hamid Karzai declared a ban on drugs after opium output reached a near-record 3,600 tons in 2003, equal to three-quarters of the world supply. Over the next two years, despite several hundred million dollars of foreign support, production increased to 6,200 tons of opium, a level estimated to exceed global demand by 30%.[126]

Loss of Entire Generations of Youth

As a result of the drug war, we have decimated generations of our youth by arresting and imprisoning them for

---

[123] "War on Drugs", Wikipedia <http://en,wikipedia.org/War_on_drugs> 24 April 2013
[124] Ibid
[125] Ibid
[126] Ibid

drug use or simple possession. Their behavior is no different than the kinds of experimenting with alcohol that older adults today engaged in the 50s, 60s and 70s. The only difference is people in those eras they didn't have to worry about getting sent to federal or state prison for three or four years. Since young people with a record find it very difficult to find employment, many give up trying and go back to drugs or turn to a life of petty crime or take the kind of menial jobs that are the only ones available for people with records. Consequently, we carved these young people out of mainstream society, denied them a full employment opportunity and left them on life's trash heap. In the process we are creating a fairly large and permanent sub-class of citizens who live on the margins. And for what reason? Making the same kind of dumb decisions that today's older generation made in times past.

Over the life of the Drug War, we have arrested, incarcerated and destroyed the lives of millions of young people who had years of productive life ahead of them, not for committing a violent crime, but for simple drug use or possession. They have been put in the company of hardened career criminals. Prison and hard core convicts become the only life and family they know for three, four or more years and prison becomes their training ground. Their "education" is to be exploited by predatory inmates.

What they learn is that the strong prey on the weak. To survive one must transform themselves from a human being into an animal – or perish. Worse, their lives have been destroyed and there is no second chance. When released, they now have a record – making it almost impossible for them to find honest work. Consequently, many end up employing the "training" they received behind bars. With a prison record they can't vote, get a job or make a decent living. When returned to the streets, they are embittered, cynical and saddest of all, they have lost hope. Thanks to a misplaced "tough on crime" mentality, this is the price one pays for being young, human and making a mistake.

One of the most shameful aspects of the Drug War is the toll it has taken on black youth. Many people fully believe that blacks are the predominant buyers and users of drugs. That is another myth that needs to be dispelled. Blacks constitute about 12% of the total U. S. population and 15% of the drug users but account for 75% of those incarcerated for drug use. Although whites represent approximately 75% of the drug using population, they constitute barely 10% to 15% of those imprisoned for drug use.[127] One of the reasons for this disparity was a 1986 law that imposed the same five year minimum sentence for possessing *five grams* of crack cocaine (popular among blacks) as for having *500 grams* of powder cocaine (favored by the white middle class), for a ratio of 100:1. The low five gram threshold meant that crack offenses were punished more severely than any other type of drug offense and was the only drug that carried a mandatory minimum sentence for simple possession. Data from the United States Sentencing Commission show that the average crack cocaine defendant received an average sentence of 129 months in 2008, or almost four years longer than the 86 month sentence for powder cocaine defendants.[128] Several years ago that ratio as reduced to about 18:1 and a mandatory minimum sentence of five years for first time conviction for possessing crack cocaine was eliminated.[129]

Destabilization of Economies and National Governments

The sheer tide of dollars flowing into countries from international drug trafficking can and has destabilized the economies and governments of a number of countries:

---

[127] "War on Drugs", Wikipedia
[128] Statement of Ricardo H. Hinojosa, Acting Chair, United States Sentencing Commission Before the
   Senate Committee on the Judiciary Subcommittee on Crime and Drugs, April 19, 2009. p. 5
[129] Steven L. Taylor, "Change in Sentencing: Crack v. Powder Cocaine", Outside the Beltway, July 29,
   2010, http://www.outsidethebeltway.com/change-in-sentencing-crack-v-powder-cocaine
   9 May 2013

"The widespread existence of corruption engenders a lack of confidence among law enforcement agencies....Ruthless trafficking organizations, with deep pockets for bribes and a demonstrated readiness to use violence, have penetrated the highest reaches of government of some nations. Corruption weakens the rule law, erodes democratic institutions, and sometimes threatens the lives of officials.[130]

The *World Drug Report 2010*, contains a chapter on the destabilizing effect of drug trafficking in transit countries. Underdevelopment and weak governance attract crime which, in turn, deepens instability. It states that the wealth, violence and power of trafficking can undermine the security and even the sovereignty of States.[131]

As a country, we, along with other civilized nations, lived for almost 40 years under the cloud of the Cold War and the fear of nuclear war with Russia. Allowing ruthless drug syndicates to become transnational, global enterprises with the money and power to overthrow national governments, at least figuratively, if not literally, makes the fear and dangers we lived with during the Cold War seem like child's play. What we are facing is the greatest menace to democracy, world peace and the rule of civilized law in the history of mankind.

---

[130] "International Drug Control Cooperation", United Nations Office of Drug Control Policy, 1999 National Drug Control Strategy. < https://www.ncjrs.gov/ondcppubs/publications/policy/99ncds/iv-h.html> 5 May 2012
[131] "World Drug Report 2010: drug use is shifting towards new drugs and new markets", United
  Nations Office on Drugs and Crime, June 23, 2010
<http://www.unodc.org/en/frontpage/2010/
  June/drug-use-is-shifting-towards-new-drugs-and-new-markets.html> 26 April 2013

Narco-terrorism is the use of illicit drugs to advance political agendas, fund terrorist activities and launch organized assaults against political authority. [132] It is also a means for destabilizing nations through violence and corruption, such as Colombia, Peru, Venezuela, Mexico, Panama, El Salvador, Myanmar, Afghanistan, Kosovo, Algeria, Sudan, Liberia, Angola and Somalia.[133] As nations are destabilized, they become easier to control and their officials more susceptible to bribes and intimidation.

Money spent on drug use in the United States flows back to traffickers in countries like Colombia and Mexico who use the proceeds to build their power base, finance extortion, arms dealing, murder, kidnappings, bribery and expanding criminal enterprises around the world by corrupting foreign governments. The Mexican cartels, awash in cash from drug commerce, now have the manpower, firepower and technology to go toe to toe with the Mexican Army. Drug traffickers have been adept at adopting the latest and most modern technology which makes controlling their activities even more difficult. Some use electronic encryption devices whose codes have not been broken by law enforcement authorities. The globalization of finance, trade and high-tech communications have made trafficking easier to carry out and harder for traditional law enforcement processes to make any headway against.

A similar observation was made by Raphael Perl, a Specialist in International Affairs, Congressional Research Service:

> "Globalization, free trade, and the expansion of democratic regimes provide opportunity for free movement of terrorists and criminal groups worldwide......Terrorism is becoming less territorially

---

[132]   Funding Terrorism
[133]   "How does prohibition help terrorists?", <u>Canadian Foundation for Drug Policy</u>, 2001,
    <http://www.cfdp.ca/terror.htm>   5 May 2013

defined and more global in reach, and….less overtly
state-sponsored and more decentralized.
Moreover…terrorism is becoming more anonymous and
that in the future it will be increasingly driven by global
religious and ideological agendas". [134]

Destabilized nations with weakened governments riddled
with corruption, make it easier for drug syndicates to continue
expanding their lucrative trafficking business without
interference from corrupt government officials and emasculated
systems of justice and law enforcement, and in some instances,
even serving as a "shadow" government. Veteran journalist
Hugh Downs made the observation that the enormous profits
made by drug organizations has allowed them to create efficient,
well trained modern militias. In Downs' words, the effect is to
create "a department of defense to protect themselves". [135] Mr.
Downs observation is indeed cogent. In Burma, a drug lord and
former general named Khun Sa commands an army of at least
20,000 soldiers.[136]
Drug money is also the main source of funding for
international terrorist groups. We need to remember the lessons
of 9/11. If we don't want an encore from terrorist groups, we
need to cut off their funding. And Prohibition has not worked
and is not the answer. Rather, it is the problem. We still don't
get it. Without Prohibition there would be no profits from drug
trafficking and the major source of terrorist funding would be cut
off. As a result, the cartels would either wither and die or turn to
other criminal enterprises such as prostitution, smuggling jewels
or precious commodities and so forth. The exact same outcome

---

[134] "U. S. Anti-Terrorism Strategy, by Raphael Perl, June 30, 2003 U. S;
Department of State,
International Information Programs,
<http://www.iwar.org/uk/news=archive/2003/06-30.htm>
4 May 2013
[135] Canadian Foundation for Drug Policy
[136] Ibid

occurred when alcohol Prohibition ended. Prohibition created organized crime and the violence that comes with it. When Prohibition was overturned in 1933, the Black Market for alcohol dried up, as did the profits it generated, and violent crime plummeted. Mobs turned to other illicit avenues for making money such as prostitution, extortion and racketeering, but the profits from these endeavors came nowhere close to the Black Market for alcohol. Essentially, we tamed rampant violence and crime by legalizing alcohol.

The violence aspect of the Drug War is one that most Americans haven't a clue about. These crime syndicates are barbaric to an extent we have not seen in our lifetime. They are depraved. They are ruthless. They thrive on torture and violence and the more gruesome, the better.

In late March, 1994, Mexican drug cartels assassinated a presidential candidate, Donald Luis Colosio at a political rally in Tijuana. Shortly after the assassination, people conducting the investigation fell like flies.[137] In September 1994, a senior official of the president's party, Francisco Ruiz Massieu, was shot to death in downtown Mexico City.[138] Alfredo de la Torre Marquez, the Tijuana chief of police was ambushed by assassins with automatic weapons. His vehicle was hit by at least 100 bullets and fifty-three were found in his body.[139] In February, 1996, Sergio Armando Silva, a newly appointed Tijuana chief of the judicial police, was cut down[140]. Prosecutor Arturo Ochoa Palacios was killed while jogging.[141] Prosecutor Sergio Moreno Perez was kidnapped and murdered along with his son in May[142]. Former police commander Isaac Sanchez Perez was shot to death

---

[137] Mike Gray, "Drug Crazy", p. 138
[138] Ibid, 138-139
[139] Scott Burns, "Drugs Cast Shadow on Border Cities, *Dallas Morning News,* 2000, <http://www.map-inc.org/alert/0158.html>   7 May 2013
[140] Mike Gray, "Drug Crazy", p. 139
[141] Ibid
[142] Ibid

in July.[143] Prosecutor Jesus Romero Magana was gunned down in front of his house in August.[144] At that time, Ernesto Ibarra Santes, a close friend of slain police captain Alejandro Castaneda, took over as federal police commissioner and vowed to end corruption in the ranks. Twenty eight days later he and his aides were blow to pieces by machine gunners who pulled alongside his vehicle. [145]

A rival cartel managed to infiltrate the highest levels of a competing cartel with a small squad of men. The leader of the group wooed the wife of the head of the cartel and persuaded her to run off with him, taking her two small children as well. He also convinced her to withdraw $7 million from her bank account. Later, while having sex with her, he cut off her head and mailed it back to her husband in a hatbox. Then he took the two small children to a bridge and threw them off.[146]

In Colombia, drug traffickers assassinated five presidential candidates. They murdered 11 of 25 Supreme Court justices and killed over 3,000 members of a legal political party. They also assassinated countless policemen, judges and witnesses.[147]

If we think these narco-traffickers will not employ the same terrorist measures in this country once they have established a a foothold in the United States, we are not facing reality. They are already here.

At a drug policy conference in 1993, a former Colombian high court judge named Gomez Hurtado warned the American participants, "Forget about drug deaths, and acquisitive crime, and addiction, and AIDS. All this pales into insignificance before the prospect facing the liberal societies of the West. *The income*

---

[143]   Ibid

[144]   Ibid

[145]   Ibid

[146]   Ibid, p. 136

[147]   "Illegal Drug Trade in Colombia", Wikipedia, <http://en.wikipedia.org/wiki/illegal_drug_trade_in_ Colombia>   11 May 2013

of the drug barons is greater than the American defense budget.
With this financial power they can suborn the institutions of the
State and, if the State resists…they can purchase the firepower to
outgun it. We are threatened by a return to the Dark Ages". [148]
That statement was made 20 years ago. If anything, the cartels
are larger, have more money, are better organized and are better
armed than then.

As we shall see in the following section, this disregard
for human life is epidemic in the drug syndicates. It is an
essential ingredient of their business model. Along with bribes, it
is how they survive and co-opt legitimate institutions of
government. They cannot be taken lightly or treated like a street
gang nuisance. As they continue their stealthy invasion of every
nook and cranny of the United States, unless we can remove the
profits from their business ventures, the time may come when we
begin witnessing some of this carnage on our own streets.

Mexico

Mexico is a country on the edge of collapse. A full ten
percent of its economy is built on drug proceeds.[149] The United
States government considers Mexican cartels to be the greatest
organized crime threat to the U.S. and has already spent an
estimated $7 billion to help fund Mexico's war with the
cartels.[150] The gesture has been futile. Mexico's security
continues to deteriorate at what is almost an exponential rate.

Pressured by the U. S., former president Felipe Calderon
ran on a platform of rooting out and destroying the drug cartels.
In 2006, he launched a military style offensive. He mobilized
troops. He used the latest technology and weaponry. He hunted

---

[148]   Mike Gray, "Drug Crazy", p. 188
[149]   Fox News <http://www.foxnews.com/woekd/2010/05/13/ap-impact-years-trillion-war-of-drugd-
     Failed-meet-goals/> 24 April, 2013
[150]   "Mexican Drug War", Wikipedia

down cartels and their leaders. He even sent 7,000 troops into his home state of Michoacan.[151]

The result of Calderon's crackdown was a violent retaliation by the cartels that over the period of Calderons's presidency led to the merciless slaughter of approximately 50,000 Mexican citizens, including members of the military and police departments, judges, mayors, police chiefs, politicians, journalists, innocent Mexican civilians and cartel members themselves.

If anything, the Mexican drug empires are stronger and more powerful now than when Calderon took office. Recognizing that his hard-line position had not worked, toward the end of his term Mr. Calderon finally admitted that the time had come for an open debate about regulating drugs, presumably through decriminalization or legalization.[152]

Calderon's predecessor, Vincente Fox, was even blunter, saying "we should consider legalizing the production, sale and distribution of drugs" as a way to "weaken and break the economic system that allows cartels to earn huge profits. Radical prohibition strategies have never worked". [153]

The violence in Mexico is out of control and destroying the country:

- The Nuevo Laredo's police chief, Robert Alejandro Garza, disappeared the same day his two brothers turned up dead.[154]

---

[151] Daniel Hernandez, "Calderon's war on drug cartels: A legacy of blood and tragedy", *Los Angeles*
  Times, December 10, 2012
  <http://articles.latimes.com/2012/dec/01/world/la-fg-wn-mexico-calderon-
    Cartels-20121130> 4 May 2013
[152] Huffington Post, <http://huffingtonpst.com/gary-johnson/legalize-
marijuana> 8 May 2013
[153] Ibid
[154] "New government, old problems as Mexico suffers from criminality",
Los Angeles Times,

- Hit lists with names of police officials are commonplace in Mexican cities along the border and not infrequently these officials are gunned down in broad daylight.[155]
- Executions have been broadcast on YouTube.[156]
- Body parts are tossed onto streets and into night clubs.[157]
- Random attacks on civilians occur regularly. On September 15, 2008, two hand grenades were thrown into a crowded plaza, killing eight people and wounding 100.[158]
- Suspected cartel hitmen killed 13 high school students and two adults at a party in Juarez.[159]
- Twenty people were killed when gunmen opened fire in a bar in Monterrey. [160]
- Two dozen heavily armed gunmen burst into a drug rehabilitation clinic and killed 19 patients ranging in age from 18 to 25.[161]

<http://www.latimes.com/news/world/worldnow/la-fg-mexico-crime-20130220,0,2181151.story?

Track=ss> 4 May 2013

[155] "Mexican Drug War",< http://en.wikipedia.org/Mexican_Drug_War> 4 May 2013

[156] Ibid

[157] Ibid

[158] "Suspect tells of holding grenade", *Los Angeles Times,* <http://articles.latimes.com/2008/sep/28/

World/fg-mexico28> 7 May 2013

[159] "Factbox: Worst Attacks in Mexico's drug war", <http://www.reuters.com/assets/print?aid=

USTRE6703K020100826> 8 May 2013

[160] "At least 20 killed in Mexico bar, officials say", *Los Angeles Times,* <http://articles.latimes.com/2011/

Jul/10/world/la-fg-mexico-violence-20110710> 7 May 2013

[161] Factbox

- Suspected cartel hitmen ambushed and killed Rodolfo Torre, a popular gubernatorial candidate, and four of his aides.[162]
- The body of the mayor of Santiago, a colonial tourist town near Monterrey, was dumped on a rural road two days after being abducted from his home.[163]
- Gunmen crashed a birthday party in Torreon and using automatic weapons, killed 17 party-goers and wounding 18 others. It was later discovered that the gunmen were let out of jail by corrupt officials. The killers had used weapons and vehicles borrowed from prison guards and later returned to their cells.[164]
- Between 2006 and 2011, 46 journalists and 31 mayors have been murdered.[165]
- In the first six months of 2012, 335 policemen were murdered and at least 341 persons were known to have been decapitated.[166]
- Also in Torreon, hit men killed eight people in a bar. Four decapitated bodies were later found.[167]
- A leading political figure and former presidential candidate, Diego Fernandez de Cevallos, was kidnapped in 2010 and held hostage seven months before being released. He is the most high profile figure to have been kidnapped yet, and simply indicates how aggressive the cartels had become and how little they feared of punitive action from the government.[168]

[162] Ibid
[163] Ibid
[164] Ibid
[165] "Invasion of the Drug Cartels:, National Post,
<http://news.nationalpost.com/2012/07/13/
    Mexican-drug-cartels-spreading-influence-graphic/> 8 May 2013
[166] Ibid
[167] Ibid
[168] Ibid

- On May 13, gunmen broke into the home of Jose Mario Valera, a mayoral candidate in Valle Hermosa, killing him and his son, after Mr. Valera ignored warnings from the cartels to end his campaign. [169]
- Cartels have murdered politicians, four television journalists, three photojournalists, bloggers and Twitter users[170]
- At least one dozen Mexican musicians who perform folk songs that celebrate cartel leaders as folk heroes have been murdered.[171]

And the carnage goes on: unabated, unstoppable and unrelenting. The incidents above are only the tip of the iceberg.

Prior to the War on Drugs, the Mexican government and drug dealers had an unspoken "live and let live" policy. The government would turn a blind eye to drug selling so long as rival drug gangs kept violence between themselves to a minimum.[172] With the introduction of stricter interdiction measures along the Mexican border resulting from the War on Drugs, the United States placed increasing pressure on the Mexican government to be a more proactive partner in the drug war. Calderon took action after his election. In response to increased law enforcement efforts to curtail drug trafficking, the cartels responded by aligning interests, merging into larger cartels, acquiring technology and firepower that is probably superior to the Mexican Army, and becoming increasingly ruthless, employing terrorist tactics to subdue local citizenry and to intimidate local law enforcement.

Since Calderon declared war on the cartels in 2006, approximately 50,000 people have been killed.[173] To put that

---

[169] Ibid
[170] "Mexican Drug War", Wikipedia
[171] Ibid
[172] Wallace-Wells, "How American Lost the War on Drugs"
[173] "Mexican Drug War", Wikipedia
<http://en.wikipedia.org/wiki/Mexican_Drug_War> 4 May 3023

number in perspective, disregarding global conflicts such as the two World Wars, Korea, Vietnam and putting aside the casualties from the American Civil War, in all of the rest of America's wars – Revolutionary War, War of 1812, Indian Wars, Spanish-American War, the Philippine Insurrection, Afghanistan and both wars in Iraq - since 1776 through today, a span of 234 years, the United States has lost approximately 21,000 troops, or less than half the number of people murdered in Mexico over the past six years in drug-related violence. The city of Juarez alone has suffered 5,000 drug homicides since 2006, more than the number of American troops who have died in Afghanistan and the two Iraq wars combined.[174] It seems accurate to repeat the comment made in the opening of this book: when we speak of the war on drugs, it seems more accurate to say drugs are warring on us.

Equally debilitating is the corruption at all levels of the Mexican government, including the judiciary, which has eroded the confidence of Mexican citizens in the integrity and effectiveness of its law enforcement, military and local and federal government. Mexico's police and armed services are known to be contaminated by multimillion dollar bribes from the trans-national narco-trafficking business and are widely considered to have attained the status of a national security threat.[175]

Some agents of the Federal Investigations Agency are believed to work as enforcers for the Sinaloa cartel. The Mexican attorney general reported in late 2005 that nearly 1,500 of AFI's 7,000 agents were under investigation for suspected criminal activity.[176] Purges have been implemented by the federal

---

[174] "United States Casualties of War", Wikipedia <http://en.wikipedia.org/wiki/United_States_Casualties_ Of_War> 24 April, 2010

[175] "Mexican Drug War", Wikipedia

[176] "Policia Federal Ministerial", Wikipedia, <http://en.wikipedia.org/wiki/Federal_Investigatons_ Agency> 4 May 2013

government of police forces in Nuevo Laredo, Michoacan, Baja California and Mexico City. In 2007, president Calderon purged 284 federal police commanders from all 31 Mexican states and the Federal District. Some of the high profile arrests included the chief of the federal police, two former chiefs of the Organized Crime Division and the ex-director of Mexico's Interpol office.[177]

Under "Operation Cleanup", carried out in 2008, several agents and high ranking officials were arrested and charged with selling information or protection to cartels. A member of Mexico's lower house of congress was discovered to be a high ranking member of La Familia Michoacana drug cartel.[178] After Calderon deployed federal forces to Juarez , the homicide rate actually increased as did kidnappings.[179]

The drug violence in Mexico has widened and is crossing the border. The Department of Homeland Security is considering using National Guard troops to prevent drug violence from spreading into the U. S. The governors of Texas and Arizona have asked the federal government to send additional National Guard troops to help seal the border and to the halt the spreading violence in border communities in both states from the violence of drug cartels.[180]

Former presidents of Brazil, Mexico and Colombia said the U. S. drug war is pushing Latin America into a downward

[177] "Latin America: Mexico Purges Federal Police Chiefs in Drug Corruption Review", StoptheDrugWar,,
   <http://stopthedrugwar.org/print/6312>   4 May, 2013

[178] "2 Mexican politicians sought; drug cartel link alleged, CNN.com/World,
<http://edition.cnn.com/
   2009/WORLD/Americas/07/15/mexico.violence/index.html> 4 May 2013
[179] John MacCormack, "Drug War is Killing Mexico border cities". *San Antonio News,* March 27, 2010,
   <http://www.mysantoni
o.com/news/Drug_war_is_killing_Mexico_border_cities.html> 7 April 2010
[180] "Mexican Drug War", Wikipedia

spiral. Former President Cardoso of Brazil said that the evidence showed the war on drugs a failed war.[181]

Colombia

Corruption caused by illicit narcotics trafficking is especially prevalent in Colombia. According to the international monitoring group Transparency International:

"Colombia has suffered the tragic consequences of endemic theft by politicians and public officials for ages. Entwined with the production and trafficking of illegal drugs, this behaviour exacerbated underdevelopment and lawlessness in the countryside, where a brutal war continues to claim the lives of some 3,500 civilians a year. A World Bank survey released in February 2002 found that bribes are paid in 50 percent of all state contracts. Another World Bank report estimated the cost of corruption in Colombia at $2.8 billion annually, the equivalent of 60 percent of the country's debt". [182]

In February, 2010, the Colombian government arrested Ramiro Anturi Larrahondo, a lawyer assigned to the Attorney General's Office, for receiving thousands of dollars from the Rastrojos BACRIM in return for intercepting security agency calls and feeding information back to narcotics traffickers. [183]

The National Anti-Narcotics Agency (or "DNE"), is the agency in charge of handling assets seized from drugs traffickers.

---

[181] "Mexican Drug War", Wikipedia
[182] Thelma Luzzani, Transparency International, "Global Corruption Report 2001: South America (Berlin,
Germany: Transparency International 2001) p. 176
[183] United States Department of State Bureau for International Narcotics and Law Enforcement Affairs, "
"International Narcotics Control Strategy Report: Volume 1: Drug and Chemical Control (Washington, DC, March 2012), p. 175

The DNE was dismantled amid investigations into fourteen high-level political figures, including Congressmen and a former president of the Senate for irregularities. In September, 2011, the Attorney General brought charges for embezzlement, fraud and conspiracy against former DNE Director, Omar Figueroa and ten other former DNE officials.[184]

The CNP Criminal Investigative Chief of Caqueta was arrested in January 2010 for transporting over 100 kilograms of cocaine and in June, 23 police officers were arrested in two separate anti-drug sting operations. In May, seven police officers, two Navy officers and two Prosecutor General's Corps of Technical Investigators agents based in Choco department were arrested for their ties to a BACRIM (Spanish acronym for criminal gangs) organization. In the same month another three CNP officers were arrested for collaborating with the Rastrojos BACRIM. In August 2011, seven police officers and three army soldiers were arrested for allegedly being on the payroll of a deceased BACRIM leader. Former Defense Minister Rodrigo Rivera subsequently announced that 100 policemen were under investigation for their ties to the Rastrojos BACRIM.

The Presidential Programme Against Corruption in Colombia specifically addresses 'narco-corruption':

> "Colombia…is particularly poisoned by the interplay of narcotics and violence, with an estimated one million people internally displaced as a result of battles for territorial control by rebel groups and paramilitary forces. The corruptive effect of this kind of profit is devastating, since it has penetrated to perverse levels within the judiciary and the political system". [185]

---

[184] Ibid
[185] Transparency International (Berlin, Germany: Transparency International, 2003), p. 108

The official report of the Presidential Programme concluded:

> "...the rapid accumulation of wealth from illegal drugs has fostered codes and behaviors which promoted corruption, fast money and the predominance of private welfare over general interest". [186]

Central America

Although a fairly recent entrant, Central America is now on the front lines of the drug trade. Virtually all cocaine headed for the U. S. now passes through Guatemala. Mexican cartels have become active through much of Central America. [187]As well as using it as a corridor, the traffickers are moving more of their operations to Central America. The president of Costa Rica says rather than being simply a transit route, Central America now produces and processes drugs. One reason is the amount of largely uninhabited areas that make ideal locations for manufacturing and distribution of drugs and for other organized crime activities. There simply is not enough manpower to patrol the nation's extensive forests. The Peten is a large, sparsely populated jungle region in northern Guatemala. Because of its isolated location, it has become an ideal area for clandestine flights from other drug producing states such as Colombia and Venezuela. There is so much money generated that the planes are considered disposable.[188]

The other appeal to drug traffickers of relocating more of their operations to Central America is weak law enforcement, poverty and governments still in turmoil after decades of civil

---

[186] Thelma Luzzani, p. 176
[187] "The tormented isthmus", *The Economist,* <
http://www.economisst.com/node/185582564>
        11 May 2013
[188] Ibid

wars.[189] The Golden Triangle region of Guatemala, Honduras and El Salvador has become one of the chief engines of the drug trade and with it, has the highest murder rates in the world. [190]

` **El Salvador**

During the presidency of president Calderon, Mexican cartels began outsourcing some of their operations to Central America. The Zetas and the Sinaloan cartels were among the first to make this change. The police chief of San Salvador, the capital city, states that the Mexican cartels are hiring street gangs known for their violence to do their enforcement work for them. The gangs are employed as hit men to serve the cartel's need for revenge murders.[191]

The country also has its own drug syndicates. The largest is called the Cartel de Texis which controls a large swath of land in the northern part of El Salvador. The editorial director of the El Salvadoran news website says,

> "The power of the cartels is increasing. The drug traffic is increasing. Because they own policemen, judges, congressmen, local mayors, they basically manage their piece of territory as their own. So they charge drug cartels for crossing their territory free of threats from security forces".[192]

A researcher at the University of Central America who studies violence in El Salvador says unequivocally that organized

---

[189] Ibid

[190] Ibid

[191] Jason Beaubien, "El Salvador Grapples With Upswiing In Drug Traffic", NPR Radiio, May 31, 2011
    <http://www.npr.org.'2010/05/31/136727186/el-salvador-grapples-with-upswing-in-drug-traffic>
    11 May 2013

[192] Ibid

crime is intensifying. She points out that the homicide rate has doubled since 2003 and ancillary crime such as extortion and kidnapping is on the rise. She says, "The state, the institutions for security and justice, have been penetrated by organized crime for many years and this has blocked the state from effectively pursuing these criminals". In fact, she says that one of the gravest dangers facing the country is that organized crime is substituting for the legitimate functions of government".[193]

In the first three months of 2009, an average of nearly 12 people a day were murdered.[194] This tiny country of only 7 million had a homicide rate five times that of Mexico and ten times that of the U. S.[195] One of the nation's leading human rights organizations has analyzed homicides every year since 2004. They determined that not all homicides were committed by drug gangs but by rogue police officers, private security guards and people hired simply to be hitmen.

Honduras

Honduras serves as a key smuggling port for Mexican drug cartels which they use to expand trafficking networks into Central America. Along with several other Central American countries, Honduras has become a transshipment point for U. S.–bound illegal drugs, predominantly cocaine. Honduran officials say the northern coast of Honduras serves as a drug pipeline connected to the U. S.[196]

---

[193] Ibid
[194] Tracy Wilkinson, "El Salvador grapples with rising bloodshed", *Los Angeles Times,* May 13, 2009,
    <http://www.articles.latimes.com/2009/may/13/world/fg-salvador-murders13>   11 May 2013
[195] Ibid
[196] "Drugs and Violence Underscore U. S. Influence in Honduras", Inter Press Service, June 28, 2012.
    <http://www.ipsnewsnews.net/2012/06/drugs-and-violence-underscor-u-u-influence-in-honduras/>
    11 May 2013

Drug traffickers fleeing crackdowns in Colombia and Mexico have flooded into Honduras. Central America now serves as the crossing point for 84% of all shipments of cocaine destined to the U. S.[197]

As has been the case everywhere the drug trade operates, Honduras has become one of the most violent nations on earth. Its homicide rate in 2010 was 82 homicides for every 100,000 people, the highest rate in the world.[198]

Funding Terrorism

Perhaps the most frightening but least understood aspect of the Drug War is the connection and interaction between drug cartels and international terrorist groups. Profits from drug trafficking is the blood money that funds terrorist organizations. Al Qaeda, Hamas, Hezbollah, The Palestinian Islamic Jihad, Shining Path and the Revolutionary Armed Forces of Columbia (FARC), the IRA, and Chechens in Russia are but a few,[199] but all use money from drug sales to finance their political agenda and terrorist activities. Of twenty-eight international terrorist organizations identified by the U. S. State Department in 2001, at least twelve were involved in drug trafficking.[200] The number is believed to be even higher today.

---

[197] Ibid

[198] Ibid

[199] "Rachael Ehrenfeld, Director, American Center for Democracy & the New York City Center for the
    Study of Corruption and the rule of Law (CSC), New York, USA, "Funding Terrorism: Sources and
    Methods", 2002, Workshop held at Los Alamos National Laboratory March 25-29, 2002

[200] Asa Hutchison, DEA Administrator, Testimony Before the Senate Judiciary Committee Subcommittee
    On Technology, Terrorism and Government Information, March 13, 2002 <http://2001-2009.state.gov/
    p/inl/rls/rm/9239.htm> 4 May 2013

Reuters News Agency quoted Interpol's chief drugs officer, Iqbal Hassain Rizvi as far back as 1994, as saying that "drugs have taken over as the chief means of financing terrorism". [201]

For criminal organizations, drugs are simply a lucrative business endeavor. However, for terrorist groups, profits from drug sales feed the terrorist lifeline. It is their most vital and dependable source of funding.[202] It is a means for raising money to finance their insurgent actions. The crackdown on traditional sources of financial assistance due to enhanced security and monitoring of international financial transactions has greatly reduced the historical sources of funds into terrorist organizations. As a consequence, such groups are increasingly relying on drug trafficking for financial aid.

In 2003, Raphael Perl, a specialist in international affairs for the U. S. Congressional Research Service, gave a talk in Berlin on "U. S. Anti-Terrorism Strategy". In his talk he warned of the increased likelihood of terrorist groups seeking funding from trafficking organizations:

"In the wake of September 11th, the international community has placed emphasis on curbing financing of terrorist groups, as has dramatically enhanced efforts to limit and seize sources of terrorist funding. This has spawned renewed focus on the narcotics trade as a source of funding for such groups. Even in instances where groups do not actively work together, the synergy of their

---

[201] "How Does Prohibition help terrorists?", Submission to the Senate of Cancda Special Committee on
    Illegal Drugs, October 29, 2001, Canadian Foundation for Drug Policy, <http://www.cfdp.ca/
    terror.htm> 5 May, 2012
[202] Rachael Ehrenfeld

separate operations and shared efforts at destabilization pose an increasing threat". [203]

He made clear the strategy it would take to eliminate the threat of terrorists and drug traffickers working together:

"...a desired end state where the scope and capabilities of global terrorist organizations are downscaled to the extent that they become localized, unorganized, un-sponsored, and rare enough that they can be almost exclusively dealt with by criminal law enforcement. To accomplish this mission, emphasis is placed on international action by working with the willing, enabling the weak, persuading the reluctant, and compelling the unwilling"[204]

In other words, we need to take seriously the threat of an interdependent relationship between terrorist groups and drug organizations and be prepared to do whatever it takes to reduce the power and influence of cartels. While he didn't say so, legalizing drugs is certainly one of the quickest ways to emasculate the cartels.

Drug trafficking helped the Taliban regime stay in power during the late 1990s. The DEA estimated that the Taliban collected more than $40 million a year in profits from the opium trade. Some of the cash went to terrorist groups operating out of Afghanistan.[205] In 2008, a United Nations report indicated that amount to be more in the range of $75 million to $100 million. The report further stated that in the 2005-2008 period, the

---

[203]   Raphael Perl, "U. S. Anti-Terrorism Strategy", U. S. Department of State, International Information

    Programs, June 30, 2003 <http://www.iwar.org.uk/news-archives/2003/06-30.htm>   4 May 2013

[204]   Ibid

[205]   Ted Galen Carpenter, "How the Drug War in Afghanistan Undermines America's War on Terror",

    Foreign Policy Briefing, No. 84, November 10, 2004.

cumulative revenue accruing to the Taliban was even higher, estimated at $350 to $650 million, or about $90 million to $160 million a year. [206]

In Colombia, FARC is active in cultivating drugs on their own, but also taxing drug traffickers. It is believed that FARC earns approximately one billion dollars a year from their drug enterprise and maybe twice that amount.[207]

Drug traffickers and terrorist groups have linked into a mutually beneficial relationship based on a classic division of labor. The terrorist organization may control the territory where the drugs are cultivated and harvested and the criminal elements run the trafficking operations. Each protects the other from law enforcement or governmental intrusion.

Unfortunately, as long as there is a profit to be made in trafficking drugs, the links between drug cartels and terrorists will only strengthen which is not in the best interests of the United States or the international community. International drug cartels and terrorist organizations pose an increasing menace, either separately or working in concert, that has proved impossible to control, much less eliminate. The logical end of such a trend is terrorist access to and use of Weapons of Mass Destruction. We cannot underestimate such a possibility but neither can we reduce the risk if as a nation, we continue to ignore what is going on around us and more importantly, the reason why. Heightened prohibition measures have not reduced the flow of drugs, drug use, drug trafficking, crime or terrorism. All it has done is fuel the transformation of once small time drug cartels into international mega-organizations and provide incentives for them to work cooperatively with terrorist groups, a

---

[206] Drug War Facts, <http"//drugwarfacts.org/cms/?q=node/38> 9 April, 2010

[207] "FARC's Cocaine Sales to Mexico Cartels Prove Too Rich to Subdue", *Bloomberg News,*
    January 20, 2010,
<http://www.bloomberg.com/apps/news?pid=newsacrhive&sid> 11 May, 2013

recipe for ultimate disaster. The only way to extinguish these threats is to eliminate profits from the drug trade which can only happen by legalizing all drugs that are currently illicit.

CHAPTER EIGHT

The Invasion of America

The inevitable result of the War on Drugs has been the invasion of the United States by international drug cartels. Our self righteous indignation over drug use that gave birth to the drug war has backfired on us. Seeking to punish people for indulging in substances that are less harmful than tobacco and liquor has created a monstrous, ruthless juggernaut of drug terrorism that has overpowered our national systems of law enforcement, military forces and institutions of government.

Not long ago, Phoenix was named the kidnapping capital of North America with 400 such incidents and was second in the world for kidnappings, surpassed only by Mexico City.[208] Phoenix officials and law enforcement say the vast majority of the kidnappings were drug-related.

We got our war on drugs. The problem is it is we who are being warred against and we are losing the battle. As a nation we have our collective heads in the sand. Our government seems blithely uninterested in taking this threat seriously and taking logical measures against it. The American people see the drug war as a "Mexican" problem or a "Latin American" problem. The Drug Hawks are like the Hawks of Vietnam, Iraq and Afghanistan who let false bravado and phony machismo lead us into wars we were unable to "win" and had no business fighting in the first place. Once again we are paying a price for a laissez faire attitude and for letting a minority of law and order fanatics put us on a road that can lead nowhere but to national ruin.

Too many Americans are afraid to speak out against the Drug War for fear of being perceived as "bleeding heart liberals" and all the other labels favored by no-nothing groups who will

---

[208] "Phoenix, Arizona: Kidnapping Capital of the USA", Latina, <http://www.latina.com/lifestyle/news-politics/phoenix-arizona-kidnapping-capital-usa> 4 May 2013

stop at nothing to intimidate us from challenging their policies of disaster. The war on drugs is no longer a battle that will be carried out in distant locations such as Mexico, Colombia or any of the other countries that have been overrun by drug cartels. We will soon be fighting the war on drugs on American soil. Either we muster the courage as a people and demand change or we can watch our nation sink into a black hole of crime, corruption and violence as has happened with every other nation invaded by the cartels.

In February, 2013, the city of Chicago named Joaquin "El Chapo" Guzman, head of the Sinaloa drug cartel as its first "Public Enemy Number One" in almost 80 years, since Al Capone. [209] The head of Chicago's Drug Enforcement Administration office told CNN:

> "While Chicago is 1500 miles from Mexico, the Sinaloa drug cartel is so deeply embedded in the city that local and federal law enforcement are forced to operate as if they were on the border"

The "occupation" of the Windy City by the Sinaloa cartel shows the extent of the penetration into the United States by Mexican drug machines. The Associated Press and other news organizations have reported that cartel cells have been established in Atlanta, Louisville, Columbus, Ohio, and even rural North Carolina. [210]All told, all five of the major Mexican cartels have some form of presence in at least 1,200 American cities, up from 230 in 2008.[211]

---

[209] "Mapping the Incredible Spread of Mexican drug cartels in the U. S.", Foreign Policy, March 10, 2013,

<http://blog.foreignpolicy.com/posts/2013/05/02/mexican_drug_cartels_penetration_united_states>,
9 May 2013

[210] Ibid
[211] Ibid

Officials of the Texas Department of Public Safety said that the Mexican cartels were the "most significant organized threat" to the Lone Star State. [212]

United States authorities report a spike in killings, kidnappings and home invasions that have been linked to Mexican cartels. At least 19 Americans were killed in 2008 and another 92 were killed between June 2009 and June 2010. [213] The U. S. Drug Enforcement Administration reports that the Mexican drug cartels operating along our border with Mexico are more sophisticated and dangerous than any organized criminal group in U. S. law enforcement history. The cartels employ grenade launchers, automatic weapons, and have begun using roadside IEDs ("Improvised Explosive Devices") that terrorists successfully used against the U. S. military in Iraq.[214]

The F.B.I. estimates that cartels control distribution of narcotics in more than 230 U.S. cities from New England to the Southwest.[215] Mexican cartels have already established alliances with U. S. street and prison gangs to expand their distribution networks. Several years ago, the U. S. government produced the arrests of at least 345 suspected members of the notorious La Familia cartel and 755 members of the Sinaloa cartel operating on American soil.[216]

Seeking to nip in the bud the growing influence of the Sinaloa cartel in the U.S., Attorney General Eric Holder recently announced that federal agents had arrested more than 50 suspects

---

[212] "Europol: Mexican Drug cartels want a foothold in Europe", *Los Angeles Times,*
    <http://www.latimes.com/news/world/worldnow/la-fg-wn-mexico-cartels-20130412,0,2420255.story>
    4 May 2013
[213] "Mexican Drug War", Wikipedia
[214] Ibid
[215] HuffingtonPost, "Politics", <http://www.huffingtonpost.com/gary-johnson/legalize-marijuana-to-
    Sto_b_696430.html?view+print&comm._ref=false> 8 May 2013
[216] Mexican Drug War, Wikepedia,
<http://en.wikipedia.org/wiki/Mexican_Drug_War> 4 May 2013

in raids at different ends of the country – California, Maryland and Minnesota. Said Holder, "They are lucrative, they are violent and they are operated with stunning planning and precision". A DEA official said the raid showed the tentacles of Mexican crime syndicates had spread across the U. S. even to small towns like Stowe, Iowa which was used by the cartel as a conduit to funnel drugs around the country.[217]

We need to understand that these cartels are not operating by themselves or without the support of other criminal organizations native to the United States. The Mafia and other American crime syndicates have formed partnerships with the cartels for mutual profit and benefit. Indeed, one of the fears of professional law enforcement is that the two groups will increasingly interact until they evolve into a formal crime organizations that combined will transcend the power and reach of either separately.

---

[217] Delvin Barrett, *Associated Press,* "Border Violence" Drug Cartels Tentacles Stretch Across U. S.,
<http://www.cnsnews.com/news/article/border-violence-drug-cartels-tentacles-stretch-across-us> ,
4 May 2013

CHAPTER NINE

What is the Solution?

By any measure, the War on Drugs has been a catastrophic and expensive failure that is wreaking havoc on a global scale. Despite spending hundreds of billions over the past 40 years, despite an estimated 19,000 federal, state and local law enforcement officials dedicated to the drug war on a full-time basis, despite the addition of 1,000 prisons in the last 20 years, and despite over one half million citizens behind bars for non-violent drug violations, we are no closer to keeping illicit drugs out of the country or persuading Americans not to use drugs than we were 40 years ago.

The only conclusion we can reach as a society is that we cannot justify the war on drugs for a number of reasons:

- It isn't producing results.
- It is based on misconceptions and flawed premises.
- It is contributing to the global disruption of economies and governments.
- It has provided the primary financial support of international terrorist organizations.
- It has given rise to powerful and almost invincible drug trafficking organizations we have been helpless to stop
- It is contributing to brutal violence that continues to intensify and spread
- It is prejudicial, inhumane and needlessly destroying human lives
- It is cost ineffective and cost prohibitive.
- It is corrupting systems of justice and law enforcement.

-       It has emboldened cartels to begin invading the
        United States and set up drug trafficking cells
        border to border and coast to coast.
-       There are better alternatives.

Basically, we are flushing billions of dollars a year down the toilet, along with millions of our citizens and young people, simply to satisfy the mentality of the law and order crowd and to help politicians, who have become experts at pandering to our fears, get elected.

The drug war has claimed more victims as a by-product than it has saved by design. The definition of insanity is doing the same thing over and over and expecting a different result. We have invested hundreds of billions of dollars in a program that has produced a zero return – it's accomplished absolutely nothing. With almost 752,000 deaths each year from heart disease and strokes and roughly 600,000 from cancer, those dollars would have more productively been spent finding cures for these diseases. With our national debt hovering at almost two trillion dollars, money spent on the drug war could have been used to help rescue our economy. It is has been estimated that over two trillion dollars of drug money is being laundered each year.

As a civilized society, we must ask ourselves some hard questions. Exactly what is the "drug menace" we are fighting?

As the evidence shows, drugs can be less addictive than cigarettes and alcohol which cause infinitely more harm and suffering. Former Supreme Court Justice Byron White once said, "While the collateral consequences of drugs such as cocaine are indisputably severe, they are not unlike those which flow from the misuse of other, legal substances." Besides, if we're truly concerned with drug abuse and addiction, incarceration is not exactly the most appropriate or cost effective solution. Are we to imprison morbidly obese people who won't stop eating cheeseburgers and donuts?

Why are we treating people with serious drug problems differently than people who have serious addictions to other substances? Why are we sentencing to years in prison the person caught with a couple of grams of cocaine or a few ounces of marijuana but letting off the hook the guy who buys a fifth of Jack Daniels or a carton of Marlboros?

Presently, a growing number of professionals within the justice system, medical community and law enforcement profession are questioning whether spending billions a year to wage a war whose most noteworthy accomplishment is to fill our prisons with non-violent drug users makes sense as either social or economic policy. As noted in a 1999 Atlantic Monthly article by Eric Schlosser: [218]

"Crimes that in other countries would usually lead to community service, fines or drug treatment – or not be considered crimes at all – in the United States now lead to a prison term, by far the most expensive form of punishment".

Unfortunately, no politician has ever been elected by advocating a treatment approach to the drug problem.

The respected nationally syndicated financial columnist Scott Burns, takes a similar view. Commenting on the futility of curbing the drug flow from Mexico, he writes:

"Our 'war on drugs' is a Vietnam: Whatever we spend to complete the Tortilla Curtain and turn the entire 2,000 mile border (between Mexico and the U. S.) into an American version of the Great Wall of China, it will not be enough to stop the movement of drugs across the border or to reduce the carnage on both sides. What to do? Something radical: Eliminate the profit in illegal drug traffic.

---

[218] Schlosser

"Decriminalize the production, distribution and use of drugs. Disembowel criminal levels of profitability. Have normal levels of profitability by conventional companies that produce and distribute high-quality, low-cost drugs. Use taxes on drugs to support treatment programs. Have the *cahones,* as a nation, to realize that we are awash in substance abuse...realize that the legality/illegality of substances ranging from legal alcohol and prescription tranquilizers to illegal cocaine and heroin are transitory social consequences that allow criminals to make fortunes, to kill substance abusers and inflict agony on their loved ones". (Parenthetical added) [219]

Prominent members of the international law enforcement community had already reached the same conclusion. Some years ago, the 9th International Conference on Drug Policy Reform was held in Santa Monica, California. A keynote speaker at the conference was Dr. Joseph McNamara, a Research Fellow at Stanford University. However, Dr. McNamara is no think-tank liberal. He is a veteran of the New York City Police Department and a former Chief of Police of both Kansas City and San Jose. Dr. McNamara acknowledges the drug war is politically motivated and that politicians are afraid to confront the reality of the need for reform. As Dr. McNamara states, "It's too easy to be tougher on drugs than your opponent".[220]

The top leaders in American law enforcement, representing more than 50 agencies, participated in the Hoover Law Enforcement Summit. Some of the more interesting revelations that came from that meeting are as follows:[221]

---

[219] Scott Burns, *Dallas Morning News,* March 21, 2000
<http://www.mapinc.org/alert/0158.html>
    7 May, 2013
[220] Hoover Law Enforcement Summit, May 17, 1995
[221] Ibid

- 90% of the police leaders present repudiated the federal War on Drugs. The other 10% said they did not support it. social and medical problem. They were also unanimous in their view that expanded access to treatment and education would be far more effective than more arrests and prisons.
- Former Secretary of State under Ronald Reagan, George Shultz, denounced the War as wrong-headed and not making sense economically.
- Two federal judges spoke of the virtual implosion of our nation's court systems caused by mandatory sentencing requirements and prosecuting an increasing flood of drug cases.

Eric E. Sterling, president of the nonprofit Criminal Justice Policy Foundation says that drug violence can only be curtailed if the drug trade is regulated. According to Sterling, drug cartels cannot be eliminated since new ones are always in the wings waiting to take their place. Neither can the drug trade be stopped simply by more rigorous enforcement. Sterling states:

"Unless the present policy is redirected, we will perpetuate the same problems, tolerate the same social costs and find ourselves as we do now, no further along the road to a more rational legal and social approach than we were in 1914". [222]

An association of law enforcement officials has declared the Drug War a failure and favors legalizing drugs. Called LEAP, (Law Enforcement Against Prohibition), the group consists of 13,000 current or retired law enforcement officials, including policemen, prosecutors, wardens and judges. LEAP's mission statement says:

---

[222] Eric E. Sterling, Criminal Justice Policy Foundation

"The stated goals of current U. S. drug policy – reducing crime, drug addiction, and juvenile drug use – have not been achieved, even after nearly four decades of a policy of "war on drugs". This policy, fueled by over a trillion of our tax dollars has had little or no effect on the levels of drug addiction among our fellow citizens, but has instead resulted in a tremendous increase in crime and in the number of Americans in our prisons and jails. With 4.6% of the world's population, American today has 22.5% of the world's prisoners. But, after all that time, after all the destroyed lives and after all the wasted resources, prohibited drugs today are cheaper, stronger and easier to get than they were thirty-five years ago at the beginning of the so-called "war on drugs".

"With this in mind, we current and former members of law enforcement have created a drug-policy reform movement – LEAP. We believe that to save lives and lower the rates of disease, crime and addiction, as well as to conserve tax dollars, we must end drug prohibition. LEAP believes that a system of regulation and control of the production and distribution will be far more effective and ethical than one of prohibition. We do this in hope that we in Law Enforcement can regain the public's respect and trust, which have been greatly diminished by our involvement in imposing drug prohibition". [223]

Solutions

After forty years, we have learned, or should have learned, some lessons from the War on Drugs. The first is that heightened interdiction and enforcement efforts have had no meaningful impact on reducing drug trafficking. Simply put, it is

---

[223] Law Enforcement Against Prohibition, <http://www.leap.cc/for-law-enforcement> 25 April 2010

a physical impossibility to completely seal off our borders and coast lines or to physically inspect every person, container, ship, truck and automobile that passes through various border crossings and ports of entry. The second lesson is that increasing the penalties for drug trafficking does not serve as a deterrent. The profit margins are too high as to make the risks worth taking and for every trafficker caught and jailed, more are in line waiting to take their place. The third lesson is that making it costlier to engage in trafficking has no impact on reducing the flow of drugs. Traffickers have virtual pricing discretion and can raise prices to cover any increases in their incremental cost of business because buyers of drugs will pay whatever the going rate is. The fourth lesson is that escalating the punishments for users of illicit drugs has had no effect on curtailing demand. If people want to use drugs, they are going to do so, laws or no laws.

Logically, the only way to eliminate drug trafficking is to make it an unprofitable endeavor. This sounds easy, but the devil is in the details. The only way to remove profits from drug trafficking is the same way we removed the profits from bootlegging of alcohol and that is to legalize the sale and consumption of drugs that are now considered illegal. Pharmaceutical companies would begin manufacturing drugs that are now contraband, in compliance with FDA standards. They would be sold, presumably in drug stores. They would be regulated and taxed just as cigarettes, alcohol and prescription medications are regulated and taxed. Once that happens, the Black Market for drugs implodes because there is no longer a necessity for it. Sales and profits evaporate and drug trafficking becomes a thing of the past just like bootleggers, speakeasys and stills.

The argument to legalize drugs will meet with resistance from many sectors of society who still think of drugs and drug use in the context they have been taught to believe for half a century. It will take considerable education to dispel the myths that have surrounded the underground drug culture for decades.

Most importantly, an initiative to legalize drugs will take leadership at many levels from community grassroots organizations to the upper echelons of state and federal government. We can begin by acknowledging that drugs are not the menace that we have heard for forty years and that people have a right to use drugs just as they do alcohol, cigarettes or junk food. Neither is drug use, even recreationally, endemic within the population. As reported in the SAMHSA survey, only 9.1% of Americans used drugs in the Past Month compared to 28.1% who used tobacco and 53.2% who used alcohol. The evidence indicates that just as most people who drink are social drinkers, by the same token, most people who use drugs do so recreationally without becoming addicted.

Further, people addicted to a substance of choice should not be treated like criminals. An addiction is an addiction, regardless of the substance one is addicted to. People become addicted to drugs for the same psychological and physiological reasons they become addicted to alcohol, prescription medications, tobacco and junk food. We need to return to the practice that prevailed for decades of allowing physicians to prescribe maintenance levels of drugs to those with addictions.

Several European countries have elected a medical approach to drug addiction with apparently satisfactory results. For example, in 1997, the Swiss Federal Office of Public Health reported on the results of a three year experimental heroin maintenance program for one thousand addicts. The report showed that after three years of receiving controlled doses of maintenance-level heroin, crime among the addict population had dropped 60%, half of the unemployed addicts had found jobs, a third who had been on welfare became self-supporting, none were homeless and the general health of the group had dramatically improved. [224]

---

[224] News Briefs, September-October, 1998, Switzerland Expands Heroin Maintenance Program, Switzerland Federal Dept of Internal Affairs – Federal Office of Public Health, Unit of Drug Interventions, 3003 Berne,

The most proven effective methods for reducing abuse of any substance are education and treatment, not coercion and punishment. Cigarette smoking and alcohol consumption have shown significant declines over the last several decades, primarily as people have become better educated to the dangers of their use. The Drug War, which relies on harsh punishments, has done nothing to reduce drug use. Yet, through education alone, and without punitive measures, the smoking rate among adult Americans has dropped from between 40 to 50 percent to below 25 percent since the first Surgeon General's report on the dangers of smoking was published in 1964.

Mike Gray points out in his book that the "most successful anti-drug crusade in history was the one waged against tobacco over the past thirty years, a campaign that avoided penalties altogether. California cut smoking by 40% in a single decade by using cigarette taxes to finance anti-smoking ads". [225]

We have risen up as a nation and sent a message loud and clear to our lawmakers, judges and prosecutors that we expect them to be tough on crime. That's all well and good when it applies to perpetrators of serious crimes. However, the majority of people who use drugs are not professional criminals. Approximately three quarters of drug offenders are guilty only of simple possession. Most have never committed a violent crime in their life. Yet, these unfortunate people receive more severe punishments than murderers, rapists, burglars and pedophiles.

Because we are "tough on crime", we are throwing into prison record numbers of people who are guilty of indulging in substances that are no more harmful and substantially less lethal than other substances that are perfectly legal. Not only is this inhumane, it is the worst possible thing we could do. An increasing number of law enforcement experts – those closest to

Switzerland, Embassy of Switzerland, Roberto Balzartti, 2900 Cathedral Avenue NW,
Washington, DC
[225] Mike Gray, "Drug Crazy", p. 194

the problem - are concluding that we're not being tough on crime, we are *creating* crime and needlessly perpetuating a cycle of violence. At the same time, we are needlessly and senselessly ruining human lives.

Compelling evidence that people tend to "grow out" of drug use reinforces a medical and preventative model rather than a punitive approach. According to the SAMHSA report, the highest drug use rates are found among the 16-20 age group (who account for about 36% of total users). Rates of use then declined in each successive age group with only about one percent of persons aged 50 or older reporting current use of illicit drugs. This is a typical pattern for most forms of substance abuse – whether cigarettes, alcohol or drugs. It is the nature of young people to experiment with contraband products. However, as they mature, get jobs, marry and start families, they abandon adolescent thrills and settle down into becoming responsible citizens.

Advocates of legalization or decriminalization, are growing and they range across the political spectrum. Legalization simply does for drugs what repeal of Prohibition did with alcohol. It was made legal, regulated and taxed.

The former conservative (Republican) governor of New Mexico, Gary Johnson, gained national attention – and derision – for advocating the legalization of all drugs, from marijuana to heroin. Said Johnson, "Control it. Regulate it. Tax it. Educate people truthfully about its dangers. If we legalize it, we just might have a better society". Johnson lambasted the Drug War as "an absolute failure" that peddles "lies" in its ad campaign to youths. "They're told if they try marijuana their brains will be damaged – a kid tries it and learns that's not true. He wonders what to believe". He added, "if we put all that money (spent on the Drug War) into treatment and education, we would be a lot better off". [226]

---

[226]   Michael W. Lynch, "America's Most Dangerous Politician", Reason.com, January 1, 2001,

The organization of 13,000 law enforcement and justice system professionals who favor legalizing drugs (LEAP) underwrote a study conducted by Harvard economist Jeffrey A. Miron that was published in December 2008. The purpose of the study was to identify the economic benefits to drug legalization. Miron's study estimates that legalizing drugs would save approximately $44.1 billion a year in expenditures by federal and state governments to enforce drug prohibition. By legalizing drugs, they would be subject to being regulated and taxed just like any other pharmaceutical. Miron estimates that annual tax revenues would approximate $32.7 billion. In total, the estimated annual economic benefit to the nation from cost savings and added revenue from taxes would be about $79.3 billion.[227]

Many morally upright and religious people will have honest objections to the idea of legalizing drugs. If we stop punishing drug users, it's almost as if we are condoning their behavior, saying it's okay. But that's the wrong way to look at it. Most of us don't approve of adultery but neither do we want someone thrown in prison for having committed it. A majority of people, regardless of religious or political persuasion, would probably agree. And even if we decided to make adultery against the law, do we think it would stop?

The first hurdle to overcome is to realize that legalizing drugs isn't an endorsement of drug use any more than legalizing alcohol is an endorsement of drinking. Rather it's an acknowledgement of two basic principles. One, that adults should not be treated as criminals for indulging in a substance of their choice so long as they are doing no harm to another person. Second, that the basic property right humans have is the right to

---

<http://reason.com/archives/2001/01/01/americas-most-dangerous-politi/print > 13 May 2013
[227] Jeffrey A. Miron,, "The Budgetary Implications of Drug Prohibition", (report funding provided by
The Criminal Justice Policy Foundation), Department of Economics, Harvard University,
December, 2008

ownership of their own bodies and with it, the right to make decisions about their bodies. Whether or not it's a wise, safe or healthy choice, is a decision that adults are entitled to make nevertheless the same as over indulging on junk food, smoking five packs of Camels a day, climbing Mount Everest with no training, riding a Harley with no motorcycle experience, engaging in unprotected sex with a stranger or canoeing a class 5 whitewater rapid without a life preserver.

Once we can overcome the initial hurdle to legalization, we can begin to see the benefits. For instance, a legalized product is far easier to regulate in terms of ingredients, manufacturing, distribution and sales. One of the leading causes of drug deaths and overdoses are impurities that are mixed into drugs when they are "cut", i.e., diluted by dealers. If drugs are legalized, that risk would go away. Legal drugs would also be processed through regulated distribution channels meaning they can be traced back to the original source of purchase and manufacture. This is not true for illicit drugs. It is will also make it easier to reduce access to drugs by minors since their primary source of access would be the same as it is today for cigarettes and alcohol. While minors can always find "someone" to acquire cigarettes or alcohol for them, or to get such products from friends or family members, the controls on access by minors would be far superior than is the case with illicit drugs today.

Another benefit is that drugs sold legally would be taxed just as cigarettes and alcohol are, thereby becoming a source of tax revenue rather than being a tax drain. At the same time, we can begin to dismantle the War on Drugs apparatus at an annual savings in the hundreds of billions of dollars when we calculate the cost of added personnel necessitated by drug interdiction and law enforcement - police, sheriff's deputies, federal agents, customs agents, border patrol agents, judges, probation and parole officers, prison and jail guards, and district attorney staffs dedicated to the drug war – not to mention housing, feeding and providing medical care to the almost one million drug offenders behind bars.

To those who have moral qualms about legalizing drugs, here is a thought: if people are engaging in any activities you think are sinful and immoral, and you're truly worried about their soul, there's a better approach than throwing them in jail. Start a specialized ministry. Start a church-based outreach or rehabilitation program. Education, treatment and ministering – yes. Jail, no.

If drugs are legalized, those who are truly addicted will no longer be treated as criminals. They won't have to worry about dying from impurities mixed into their drugs by a dealer trying to stretch his inventory. They can buy drugs with a legal prescription prescribed by a physician and know that what they are buying has been regulated by the FDA. Those who cannot afford to buy would be able to get their medication from public health clinics. A young nineteen year old smoking a joint wouldn't have to worry about getting arrested and having a record follow him for the rest of his life, making it virtually impossible to find gainful employment.

The most important benefit from drug legalization will be to eliminate profits from trafficking in drugs. That one change will do more to rid the world of drug trafficking and drug related violence than all the laws, all the armies, all the prisons and all the police enforcement on the face of the planet combined. It is the only way to totally emasculate the drug cartels. The proof is Prohibition. When Prohibition was repealed and alcohol consumption made legal, the Black Market for alcohol collapsed, the mob was out of the business, prison populations were reduced and violent crime plummeted.

As Dr. Joseph McNamara has said:

> "It's the money stupid. After 33 years as a police officer in three of the country's largest cities, that is my message to the self-righteous politicians who obstinately proclaim that a war on drugs will lead to a drug-free America. About $500 of heroin or cocaine in a source country will bring as much

as $100,000 on the streets of an American city. All the cops, armies, prisons and executions in the world cannot impede a market with that kind of tax-free profit margin. It is the illegality that permits the obscene mark-up, enriching drug traffickers, distributors, dealers, crooked cops, lawyers, judges, politicians, businessmen…"

He's right.

Index

A

Afghanistan 3, 8, 9
Alexander the Great 8
Alcohol, Black Market for 6, associated with violent crime 12,
14, Use rates 21, deaths from 21 Amphetamines 9
Amyl nitrates 9
Arrests, over life of Drug War 1, for marijuana possession 15, all
drug abuse violations 25
Assassinations in Mexico, 35, Colombia 36
Asian poppy fields 17
Australia, India, legal production of heroin 3

B

Bayer 8
Borders, British Columbia, Canadian, Mexican, United States 2
Bourne, Peter 13
Brown, J. Michael 26
Buckley, William 13
Bureau of Narcotics 30,
Burma 34
Burns, Scott 50-51

C

Calderon, Felipe 36-37, 39
Calexico 30
Cannibas 9
Capone, Al 30

H

Harrison Act 10,
Hausenfaus, Eugene 29
Heroin, production 2, 3, 8, production cost and profitability 5,
discovery 8, sold by mail order 9, cough syrup ingredient 10
Holder, Eric 47
Honduras 43, homicide rate 43
Horner, Mike 30
Hurtado, Gomez, Colombian judge 34

I

Incarceration rate, U. S. versus China and USSR 2, 8, versus
other nations 24, costs per day and   annually 25, U. S. historical
24, percentage of blacks imprisoned on drug charges versus
white prisoners 24

Inhalants, use of 21-22

Interdiction, futility of 2
Invasion of America, by cartels 46-47

J

Johnson administration 30

Johnson, Gary, former governor of New Mexico 34

Juarez, homicides 39

Justice system, annual expenditures and growth of 24

K

Koop, Everett 22

L

Laudanum 8
La Familia cartel, in U. S. 47
LEAP 52, position on drug prohibition, 53

M

Mafia 3,

Marijuana, safety versus cigarettes 2, discounted as gateway drug 12, 15, properties 15, arrests for possession 25 McNamara, Joseph 22, 56

Merck 8

Meth labs 17

Mexican Army 34

Mexico, violence 35, 37-39, assassinations 35 deaths 37, 38, corruption 39, purges 39 Morphine 8

N

NAFTA 2
Nicotine, 22
Nixon 5
NSDIH 19

O

OAS 16
Office of NIH, Drug Control Policy 2
Operation Cleanup 36-39
Operation Just Cause 29

Opiates 8

P

Panama 29
Paracelsus 8
Patterson, Isabell 1
Perl, Raphael 34
Peten jungle 41
Phoenix kidnappings 45
Plan Colombia 15
Population, percentage drug use 43
Ports of entry, containers 2, 41
Prisons, growth of 24-25, new construction and cost 25,
percentage of black inmates for drug use 32 Prohibition 10,
murder rate before and after 26

Q

Quaaludes 10, 13

R

RAND corporation, study on cost effectiveness of treatment vs.
incarceration 2

S

SAMSHA 19
Schlosser, Eric 50
Schultz, George 13
Sentencing disparities, 16
Shafer Report 12
Shafer, Ray 12

www.ingramcontent.com/pod-product-compliance
Lightning Source LLC
Chambersburg PA
CBHW070549290526
45790CB00002B/614